AF708930

'Sākyamuni Buddha

...limitless, boundless, hundreds of thousands of myriads of *kotis* of Bodhisattvas Mahasattvas, as well as the four assemblies, reverently circumambulating Shakyamuni Buddha.

宣公上人德相

慈悲普度信者得救成正覺

過化存神禮之獲福悟無生

The Venerable Master Hsuan Hua

His kindness and compassion cross over all; Believers are liberated and perfect the Right Enlightenment.
Transforming beings wherever he goes, his spirit remains intact;
Those who venerate him obtain blessings and awaken to the Unproduced.

The Wonderful Dharma Lotus Flower Sutra

Volume Fourteen

Chapter Twenty:

Never-Slighting Bodhisattva

Chapter Twenty-one:

The Spiritual Powers of the Thus Come One

Chapter Twenty-two:

The Entrustment

Chapter Twenty-three:

The Former Deeds of Medicine King Bodhisattva

Chapter Twenty-four:

Bodhisattva Wondrous Sound

The Wonderful Dharma Lotus Flower Sutra

Volume Fourteen

Chapter Twenty:
Never-Slighting Bodhisattva

Chapter Twenty-one:
The Spiritual Powers of the Thus Come One

Chapter Twenty-two:
The Entrustment

Chapter Twenty-three:
The Former Deeds of Medicine King Bodhisattva

Chapter Twenty-four:
Bodhisattva Wondrous Sound

A Simple Explanation by the
Venerable Master Hsuan Hua

English translation by the
Buddhist Text Translation Society

Buddhist Text Translation Society
Dharma Realm Buddhist University
Dharma Realm Buddhist Association
Burlingame, California U.S.A.

The Wonderful Dharma Lotus Flower Sutra: Volume Fourteen

Chapter Twenty:	*Never-Slighting Bodhisattva*
Chapter Twenty-one:	*The Spiritual Powers of the Thus Come One*
Chapter Twenty-two:	*The Entrustment*
Chapter Twenty-three:	*The Former Deeds of Medicine King Bodhisattva*
Chapter Twenty-four:	*Bodhisattva Wondrous Sound*

Published and translated by:

Buddhist Text Translation Society
1777 Murchison Drive
Burlingame, CA 94010-4504

© 1998 **Buddhist Text Translation Society**
Dharma Realm Buddhist University
Dharma Realm Buddhist Association

First English edition 1998

07 06 05 04 03 02 01 00 99 98　　10 9 8 7 6 5 4 3 2 1

ISBN 0-88139-446-7

Library of Congress Catalog Card Number: 77-87782

Printed in Taiwan

Note: Pinyin is used for the romanization of Chinese words, except for proper names which retain familiar romanizations.

Contents

The Eight Guidelines of
The Buddhist Text Translation Society

1. A volunteer must free him/herself from the motives of personal fame and profit.
2. A volunteer must cultivate a respectful and sincere attitude free from arrogance and conceit.
3. A volunteer must refrain from aggrandizing his/her work and denigrating that of others.
4. A volunteer must not establish him/herself as the standard of correctness and suppress the work of others with his or her fault-finding.
5. A volunteer must take the Buddha-mind as his/her own mind.
6. A volunteer must use the wisdom of Dharma-Selecting Vision to determine true principles.
7. A volunteer must request Virtuous Elders in the ten directions to certify his/her translations.
8. A volunteer must endeavor to propagate the teachings by printing Sutras, Shastra texts, and Vinaya texts when the translations are certified as being correct.

A Few Words of Explanation

In the present volume, as in other Buddhist Text Translation Society publications, the Sutra text appears in **bold** typeface at the first, or an otherwise significant, appearance in the commentary, so the reader may quickly find an explanation of any particular phrase of the Sutra text. Verses are indicated by *italic* type. As a helpful guide to the reader, a translation of the outline of the *Wonderful Dharma Lotus Flower Sutra* compiled by Great Master Ou Yi is given in full at the beginning of the book, and the individual outline headings are shown with their corresponding passages of Sutra text thoughout the book.

Outline of *The Wonderful Dharma Lotus Flower Sutra*, Chapters 20 to 24
By Great Master Ou Yi (1599—1655)

Page Headings

Chapter Twenty

Page	Headings

Page Headings

Chapter Twenty-one

Page Headings

Chapter Twenty-two

Chapter Twenty-three

Page Headings

Verse for Opening a Sutra

The unsurpassed, profound, and wonderful Dharma,
Is difficult to encounter in hundreds of millions of eons.
I now see and hear it, receive and uphold it,
And I vow to fathom the Tathagata's true meaning.

Only in millions and millions of myriads
of eons,
Inconceivable in number,
Do the Buddhas, World Honored Ones,
Happen to speak this Sutra.
Therefore, the practitioner,
After the Buddha's passing,
On hearing this Sutra,
Should not give rise to doubts,
But should, with a single mind,
Extensively proclaim this Sutra,
So that life after life he may meet the Buddhas
And quickly realize the Buddha Way.

There was a Bodhisattva by the name of Never-Slighting.
At that time the four assemblies were attached to the Dharma.
The Bodhisattva Never-Slighting would approach them
And say to them, "I will not slight you,
For you are practicing the Way and shall become Buddhas."
Hearing that, they slighted him, slandered and reviled him,
And Never-Slighting Bodhisattva endured it all.

The Wonderful Dharma Lotus Flower Sutra

Chapter Twenty: Never-Slighting Bodhisattva

Sutra:

AT THAT TIME the Buddha told the Bodhisattva Mahasattva Great Strength, "You should now know that if someone reviles, abuses, or slanders a Bhikshu, Bhikshuni, Upasaka, or Upasika who upholds the *Dharma Flower Sutra*, he will incur great offense retribution as described above. The meritorious virtues obtained through the eyes, ears, nose, tongue, body, and mind gained by the upholder of the Sutra are also as described above.

"Great Strength, once limitless, boundless, inconceivable *asamkhyeyas* of eons ago, there was a Buddha by the name of King of Awesome Sound Thus Come One, One Worthy of Offerings, One of Proper and Pervasive Knowledge, One Perfect in Clarity and Conduct, Well-Gone One, One Who Understands the World, Unsurpassed Lord, Regulating Hero, Teacher of Gods and Humans, Buddha, World Honored One.

"His eon was named 'Apart From Decay.' His country was named 'Great Accomplishment.'

"In that world, the Buddha King of Awesome Sound spoke the Dharma for the gods, humans, and *asuras*. To those who sought to be Hearers, he spoke the Dharma of the Four Truths to take them across birth, old age, sickness, and death to ultimate Nirvana. To those who sought to be Pratyekabuddhas, he spoke the Dharma of the Twelve Causes and Conditions. For the Bodhisattvas, in order to lead them to *anuttarasamyaksambodhi,* he spoke the Dharma of the Six Paramitas, which culminates in Buddha-wisdom.

"Great Strength, the Buddha King of Awesome Sound had a life span of eons equal in number to the grains of sand in forty myriads of *kotis* of *nayutas* of Ganges Rivers.

"His proper Dharma dwelt in the world for eons equal in number to the motes of dust in a single Jambudvipa. The Dharma Image Age dwelt in the world for eons equal in number to the motes of dust in one set of four continents. After benefiting living beings, he passed into stillness.

"After the Proper and Image Dharma had become completely extinct, in this country yet another Buddha appeared, also by the name of King of Awesome Sound Thus Come One, One Worthy of Offerings, One of Proper and Pervasive Knowledge, One Perfect in Clarity and Conduct, Well Gone One, One Who Understands the World, Unsurpassed Lord, Regulating Hero, Teacher of Gods and Humans, Buddha, World Honored One. In this way, in sequence, there were twenty thousand *kotis* of Buddhas, all of the same name.

"When the first Thus Come One King of Awesome

Sound had passed into stillness, and after the extinction of his proper Dharma, during the Dharma Image Age there were Bhikshus of overweening pride who assumed great power. At that time there was a Bhikshu-Bodhisattva by the name of Never-Slighting.

"Great Strength, for what reason was he called Never-Slighting? Whomever this Bhikshu met, be it a Bhikshu, Bhikshuni, Upasaka, or Upasika, he would bow to them all and praise them, saying, 'I deeply respect all of you and dare not slight you. Why? You are all practicing the Bodhisattva Path and shall attain Buddhahood.'

"This Bhikshu did not read and recite Sutras, but specialized in making obeisance to the point that when he saw the four assemblies from afar, he would approach them, bow, and praise them, saying, 'I dare not slight you, for you shall all become Buddhas.'

"Within the four assemblies, there were some who grew irate, those with impure minds who reviled him with foul mouths, saying, 'Where did this senseless Bhikshu come from, who says "I dare not slight you" and then gives us predictions, saying we shall become Buddhas? We don't need such false predictions!'

"In this way for many years he was scolded and reviled. But he never got angry. He always said, 'You shall become Buddhas.' When he said that, those people would beat him with sticks or throw stones at him. He would run off, stand at a distance, and shout out, 'I dare not slight you, for you shall all become Buddhas!' Because he always said that, the Bhikshus, Bhikshunis, Upasakas, and Upasikas of overweening pride gave him the name 'Never-Slighting.'

"When this Bhikshu's life was coming to an end, in space he heard all of the complete twenty thousand myriad *kotis* of verses of the *Dharma Flower Sutra* previously spoken by the Buddha King of Awesome Sound. He was able to receive and uphold them all. He immediately obtained the purity of the eye and the purity of the ear, nose, tongue, body, and mind, as mentioned above. Having obtained the purity of the six senses, his life span was further increased by two million *kotis* of *nayutas* of years. He extensively spoke the *Dharma Flower Sutra* for others.

"At that time the four assemblies of Bhikshus, Bhikshunis, Upasakas, and Upasikas of overweening pride who had ridiculed him and named him Never-Slighting saw that he had gained great powers of spiritual penetrations, the power of the eloquence of delight in speech, and the power of great wholesome silence. Hearing what he said, they faithfully submitted to him and followed him. This Bodhisattva further transformed thousands of myriads of *kotis* of multitudes, causing them to dwell in *anuttarasamyaksambodhi*. When his life was over, he was able to encounter two thousand *kotis* of Buddhas, all named Brightness of Sun-Moon-Lamp. Within their Dharmas, he spoke the *Dharma Flower Sutra*. By means of these causes and conditions, he further encountered two thousand *kotis* of Buddhas, all named Cloud-like Comfort Lamp King. Within the Dharma of those Buddhas, he received, upheld, read, recited, and spoke for others of the four assemblies this Sutra, and so obtained the purity of his ordinary eye and the purity of his ear, nose, tongue, body, and mind. He spoke the Dharma in the four assemblies with a heart free of fear.

"Great Strength, the Bodhisattva Mahasattva Never-Slighting made offerings to as many Buddhas as these: revering, honoring, and praising them and planting the roots of goodness.

"He later encountered a thousand myriad *kotis* of Buddhas, and within the Dharma of all these Buddhas, he spoke this Sutra. When his merit and virtue were realized, he became a Buddha.

"Great Strength, what do you think? At that time, could the Bodhisattva Never-Slighting have been anyone else? He was none other than myself! Had I not in former lives received, upheld, read, and recited this Sutra and explained it to others, I would not have been able to gain *anuttarasamyaksambodhi* so quickly. Because in the presence of former Buddhas I received, upheld, read, and recited this Sutra and explained it to others, I quickly gained *anuttarasamyaksambodhi*.

"Great Strength, because at that time the four assemblies of Bhikshus, Bhikshunis, Upasakas, and Upasikas hatefully reviled me, for two hundred *kotis* of eons they did not encounter a Buddha or hear the Dharma or meet the Sangha. For a thousand eons they suffered great torment in the Avici Hell. Having received their punishment, they once again encountered Never-Slighting Bodhisattva, who taught and transformed them to *anuttarasamyaksambodhi*.

"Great Strength, what do you think? At that time could the four assemblies who constantly slighted this Bodhisattva have been anyone else? They were just Bhadrapala Bodhisattva and the five hundred Bodhisattvas in this assembly, Lion Moon and the five hundred

Bhikshus, and Sugatachetana and the five hundred Upasakas, all of whom are irreversible from *anuttara-samyaksambodhi*.

"Great Strength, you should know that the *Dharma Flower Sutra* greatly benefits all the Bodhisattvas Mahasattvas, causing them to arrive at *anuttarasamyaksambodhi*. Therefore, after the passing into stillness of the Thus Come One all the Bodhisattvas Mahasattvas should always receive, uphold, read, and recite this Sutra, explain it to others, and write it out."

At that time the World Honored One, wishing to restate this meaning, spoke verses, saying,

In the past there was a Buddha
By the name of King of Awesome
Sound.
With limitless spiritual powers
and wisdom,
He guided all living beings.
Gods, humans, dragons, and spirits
Made offerings to him.
After this Buddha's passing into
stillness,
When the Dharma was about to
become extinct,
There was a Bodhisattva
By the name of Never-Slighting.
At that time the four assemblies
were attached to the Dharma.
The Bodhisattva Never-Slighting
Would approach them

And say to them,
"I will not slight you,
For you are practicing the Way
And shall become Buddhas."
Hearing that, they slighted him,
Slandered and reviled him,
And Never-Slighting Bodhisattva
endured it all.
When his punishment was finished,
At the end of his life,
He got to hear this Sutra,
And his six sense faculties were purified.
By the power of spiritual penetrations,
His life span was increased,
And for the sake of others,
He vastly spoke this Sutra.
The multitudes who were attached to
Dharma
All received this Bodhisattva's
Teaching and successfully
Were led to dwell in the Buddha Way.
When Never-Slighting's life ended,
He met with countless Buddhas,
And because he spoke this Sutra,
He obtained limitless blessings.
Gradually perfecting his merit
and virtue,
He quickly realized the Buddha Way.
At that time Never-Slighting
Was indeed myself!
At that time the four assemblies

Were attached to the Dharma.
Hearing Never-Slighting's words,
"You shall become Buddhas,"
By means of those causes and
conditions
Were countless Buddhas encountered.
The multitude of five hundred
Bodhisattvas in this assembly
And the men and women of pure faith
Within the four assemblies
Are now in front of me,
Listening to the Dharma.
In former lives
I exhorted these people
To listen to and receive this Sutra,
Which is the foremost Dharma.
I instructed them
And led them to dwell in Nirvana,
And life after life, to receive and
uphold
A Sutra such as this.
For only in millions and millions
of myriads of eons,
Inconceivable in number,
Can one get to hear
The **Dharma Flower Sutra.**
And only in millions and millions
of myriads of eons,
Inconceivable in number,
Do the Buddhas, World Honored Ones,
Happen to speak this Sutra.

Therefore, the practitioner,
After the Buddha's passing,
On hearing this Sutra,
Should not give rise to doubts,
But should, with a single mind,
Extensively proclaim this Sutra,
So that life after life he may meet
the Buddhas
And quickly realize the Buddha Way.

Chapter Twenty: Never-Slighting Bodhisattva

A Simple Explanation by the Venerable Master Hsuan Hua

Sutra:

AT THAT TIME the Buddha told the Bodhisattva Mahasattva Great Strength, "You should now know that if someone reviles, abuses, or slanders a Bhikshu, Bhikshuni, Upasaka, or Upasika who upholds the *Dharma Flower Sutra,* he will incur great offense retribution as described above. The meritorious virtues obtained through the eyes, ears, nose, tongue, body, and mind gained by the upholder of the Sutra are also as described above."

D3. Mentioning the blessings and offenses incurred through faith and slander as an exhortation to propagation.

E1. Prose.

F1. Recapitulating previous chapter's information on offenses and blessings.

Commentary:

Who is "Never Slighting?" He's a Bodhisattva. Is that his real name? No, it's actually a kind of nickname. He was given this name because he bowed to everyone he met. The arrogant Bhikshus, Bhikshunis, Upasakas, and Upasikas gave him the name "Never Slighting."

"Get a load of him," they would sneer. "That's Never-Slighting Bodhisattva!" Don't think that was his real name. Actually, Never-Slighting Bodhisattva was Shakyamuni Buddha in a former life when he was practicing the Bodhisattva Path. At that time he bowed to everyone, and arrogant people would ridicule him, "Hey! It's Never-Slighting Bodhisattva!" He would always say to people, "I don't dare slight you, because you will all become Buddhas." And so the arrogant Bhikshus called him Never-Slighting. Even though the name was given to him to make fun of him, he accepted it.

We shall now use the Four Siddhantas to explain his name:

1. Mundane Siddhanta. Inwardly, Never-Slighting Bodhisattva embraced both the attitude of never slighting anyone and the wisdom of never slighting anyone. Outwardly, he practiced the conduct of reverence. In all circumstances he was reverent and respectful. So I have written a verse:

Everything's a test,
To see what you will do;
Mistaking what's before your eyes,
You have to start anew!

Never-Slighting Bodhisattva recognized what was before his eyes, and so he took up the practice of bowing to people. That belongs to the category of mundane Siddhanta.

2. Siddhanta for the Sake of Others. He genuinely practiced the conduct of not slighting other people. That was Siddhanta for the sake of others.

3. Siddhanta as a Cure. With his mouth, he expounded the teaching of never slighting. He always said, "I don't dare slight you, because you will all become Buddhas." That was Siddhanta as a cure for arrogance and pride.

4. Siddhanta for the Sake of the Primary Principle. He always held an attitude of never slighting others. That was Siddhanta for the sake of the primary principle.

At that time, when the Buddha had finished the chapter "The Merit and Virtue of a Dharma Master" and was about to begin the chapter "Never-Slighting Bodhisattva," **the Buddha told the Bodhisattva Mahasattva Great Strength.** When this Bodhisattva moves his hands or takes a step, the earth quakes in six ways. As long as he stays still, nothing happens. But as soon as he moves, even just to take a single step, the world experiences six types of earthquakes. The earthquakes represent the extent of his prowess and might. The Buddha said to him, "**You should know that if someone reviles, abuses, or slanders a Bhikshu, Bhikshuni, Upasaka, or Upasika who** receives, **upholds**, reads, recites, explains, or writes out **the *Dharma Flower Sutra*, he will incur great offense retribution as described above**"— which is a monstrous retribution. How great? As big as Mount Sumeru. **The meritorious virtues obtained through the** purity of the **eyes, ears, nose, tongue, body, and mind gained by the upholder of the Sutra are also as described above.** This is as described in the previous chapter. You should be clear that the offenses belong to the one who slanders, and the merit and virtue belong to the one who upholds the Sutra; don't misinterpret the text!

Sutra:

> **"Great Strength, once limitless, boundless, inconceivable *asamkhyeyas* of eons ago, there was a Buddha by the name of King of Awesome Sound Thus Come One, One Worthy of Offerings, One of Proper and Pervasive Knowledge, One Perfect in Clarity and Conduct, Well-Gone One, One Who Understands the World, Unsurpassed Lord, Regulating Hero, Teacher of Gods and Humans, Buddha, World Honored One."**

F2. Illustrating retributions for faith and slander in the distant past.
G1. The origins.
H1. The first Buddha.
I1. Period of time.
I2. The Buddha's name.

Commentary:

Great Strength, once limitless, boundless, inconceivable *asamkhyeyas* of eons ago, there was a Buddha by the name of King of Awesome Sound. "*Asamkhyeya*" means "uncountable," and so to conceive of the number of eons that have transpired is beyond the power of imagination. "Awesome" means that he had great power. The sound of his voice was such that when he spoke, the three thousand great thousand world system trembled. He had an awesome voice. When he spoke the Dharma, people would on the one hand be afraid and on the other hand really want to listen. Because they were filled with awe and respect, they didn't dare disobey the rules, to say nothing of falling asleep during the lectures. They didn't even dare move! They would sit and listen to the Sutra lectures as if they were in samadhi, on their best behavior: no goofing around, no fidgeting or being a fussbudget, no nodding off, or any of that. Why were they so attentive? Because of the sound of this Buddha's voice. It wasn't like when I lecture: I lecture the Sutra, and you sleep. "What did he say? I'm kind of fuzzy. It's inconceivable, whatever it was." "Inconceivable" just means you have no idea what I said, because you were sound asleep. If you had heard it, it would also be inconceivable but in a different way. But I'm not Awesome-Sound, and so when I speak the Dharma, you fall asleep. If it were Awesome-Sound Buddha lecturing the Dharma, no one would dare fall asleep.

Thus Come One. Riding on the Way which is "Thus", he "came" to attain Proper Enlightenment. **One Worthy of Offerings**. A Buddha is worthy of offerings from gods and humans. **One of Proper and Pervasive Knowledge**. There was nothing he does not know. **One Perfect in Clarity and Conduct**. His wisdom was full, and his cultivation was perfected. He was called **Well-Gone One** because he could go to the very best place. **One Who Understands the World**. In the whole world, he was the one with the greatest understanding. **Unsurpassed Lord**. No one in the world possessed more knowledge and learning than he did. **Regulating Hero, Teacher of Gods and Humans, Buddha**. A Buddha has perfected the three kinds of enlightenment and is replete with the myriad virtues. **World Honored One.** He had the Buddha's ten titles, and so he was called the World Honored One.

Sutra:

"His eon was named 'Apart From Decay.' His country was named 'Great Accomplishment.'"

13. His eon and his country.

Commentary:

His eon was named "Apart From Decay," apart from all marks of deterioration and all unlucky circumstances.

What was the name of his country? It wasn't the United States, England, Italy, or Spain. **His country was named "Great Accomplishment."** Where was it? It was right where it was. If you want to go there, first you have to study the Buddhadharma. When you understand the Buddhadharma, you can go there. You won't have to buy a plane ticket, either.

A couple held their wedding here at the Buddhist Lecture Hall today. I remember when my disciple Guo Rong had his wedding here, it nearly influenced one of my left-home disciples to return to lay life. Today maybe there are some lay disciples who will be influenced to leave the home-life. Why? That is an inconceivable state, but it's not too hard to figure out. There's another kind of state, which is that the single men and women will start getting anxious. Either they'll think, "I should hurry up and do this, too," or else they'll think, "I don't want to do that. I'm going to take my time." There are many different kinds of influences and situations. These are causes planted during the "limitless, boundless *asamkhyeyas* of eons" mentioned earlier in the Sutra, and they have come to fruition today. These are inconceivable causes and inconceivable fruits. But my telling you this is the same as not telling you. You shouldn't think there is really some inconceivable state here. Actually it's all very simple, but there were a few flaws. The parents of the bride had their seats, but there was no place for the parents of the groom to sit. That made it seem like the Buddhist Lecture Hall was not being fair. It also made you American monks and nuns look irresponsible and sloppy in the way you do things. I didn't know who all the people were, but you all should have known and you didn't. I think maybe the parents of the groom were a little upset about not being treated equally. In the future you should pay more attention to these matters. They may be details, but they make a big difference. If we had treated them equally, I'm sure they would have been very happy. Some people are thinking, "It's not only the American monks and nuns who were irresponsible, the laypeople were also to blame. The laypeople should also take part of the responsibility for the things that were done wrong."

Sutra:

> **"In that world, the Buddha King of Awesome Sound spoke the Dharma for the gods, humans, and *asuras*. To those who sought to be Hearers, he spoke the Dharma of the Four Truths to take them across birth, old age, sickness, and death to ultimate Nirvana. To those who sought to be Pratyekabuddhas, he spoke the Dharma of the Twelve Causes and Conditions. For the Bodhisattvas, in order to lead them to *anuttarasamyaksambodhi,* he spoke the Dharma of the Six Paramitas, which culminates in Buddha-wisdom."**

14. Speaking the Dharma.

Commentary:

In the eon Apart from Decay, in the country called "Great Accomplishment," **in that world the Buddha King of Awesome Sound spoke the Dharma for the gods, humans, and *asuras*.** He taught the gods to cultivate the five precepts and the ten good deeds. He taught the *asuras* to cultivate precepts, samadhi, and wisdom and to put to rest greed, hatred, and stupidity. He did that because *asuras* don't keep the precepts or cultivate samadhi or wisdom. All they do is indulge in greed, hatred, and stupidity. These three poisons dominate all of their thoughts. They love to indulge in hating and in getting angry. They get greedy for something and then, if they can't have it, they get mad. Once they get mad, they become foolhardy. Then they go around picking fights with people. Why are the *asuras* greedy? Because they are never satisfied. If they don't have something they want, they scheme to get it. Once they've got it, they are afraid they're going to lose it. If they don't get it, they have afflictions. If they do get it, they also have afflictions. Either way, it's trouble, and so they're angry all day long. No matter what happens, they get angry. Once they get angry, they lose their wisdom, and as a result they lose their samadhi and their precepts. For the *asuras*, then, the Buddha King of Awesome Sound speaks the Dharma, saying, "Cultivate precepts, samadhi and wisdom. Put to rest greed, hatred, and stupidity."

Asuras are those who love to fight. "*Asura*" is Sanskrit and means "ugly." They are deformed and hideous. Their facial features are all pushed together in their face. This is not the interpenetration of the six sense faculties, either.

With the interpenetration of the six faculties, one's eyes can hear, one's ears can see, and so forth. Each faculty has the functions of all six. That ability is gained through cultivation. The *asuras'* eyes, ears, nose, and tongue are all pushed together into one place. For example, their eyes might be below their nose or their mouths might be in between their nose and eyes. They are so twisted and deformed that you can hardly call them eyes, ears, noses, or mouths. *Asuras* are unreasonable, too. When they were people, they always glared and knitted their eyebrows together so that they stood up vertically instead of spreading across horizontally. Then, when they turned into *asuras*, their facial features all got lumped together. Their appearance is very ugly, and their minds are also ugly. Their hearts are not at all proper or kind. Rotten thoughts run through their hearts all day long. They are always trying to ruin everything. The one they dislike the most is the Jade Emperor—Lord God. When they see him, they are overcome with fits of jealousy. *Asuras* fight, scold, beat, and kill people all day long. People you see on the street who yell at others, beat, or even kill people—they are all *asuras*. Thieves are yin *asuras*; soldiers are yang *asuras*.

To those who sought to be Hearers, he spoke the Dharma of the Four Truths. What are the Four Truths? They are: suffering, accumulation, extinction, and the Way. Hearers are one of the Two Vehicles. The Two Vehicles are also called the Small Vehicle, because they are satisfied with small accomplishments. They don't care to go forward and seek the Great Vehicle. They obtain certification to the first, second, third, or fourth stage of Arhatship and think that they have finished their work in the Way. They think they don't need to undergo further existence on the wheel of suffering, the wheel of birth and death, and so they don't go forward to seek the Buddha Way. We say that, "Above, they do not pursue the Buddha Way, and below, they do not save living beings." They say, "Why do I need to save living beings? Save yourself! Save your own living beings within yourself." Because they awoke to the Path when they heard the sound of the Buddha's voice, they are called Hearers.

The Buddha taught them the Four Holy Truths, the first of which is suffering. How many kinds of suffering are there? There are limitless sufferings. We also speak of three sufferings and eight sufferings. These are just general categories, however. In reality, there are infinite varieties of suffering. You could never count them all.

"But where does suffering come from?"

Suffering comes from happiness.

"Where does happiness come from?"

Happiness comes from suffering. Without suffering, there is no happiness; without happiness, there is no suffering. So I often say,

> *To endure suffering is to end suffering.*
> *To enjoy blessings is to diminish one's blessings.*

What are the three sufferings? They are:

1. The suffering within suffering
2. The suffering of decay
3. The suffering of process

The first is the suffering within suffering. Originally, let's say someone is poor, but then on top of that he has no home to live in, no food to eat, and no clothes to wear. That is suffering added on to suffering.

"Poor people might suffer, but rich people don't!" you might say.

No, wealthy people also suffer. There is the suffering of decay when you lose what you had. Say, for example, a forest fire roars through an area of exclusive housing in a canyon and burns it to the ground. These people weren't suffering from poverty by any means, but now they are poor. That is the suffering of blessings and honor gone bad.

"There's suffering in being poor and in being wealthy. Well, I'm neither one, so I'm not suffering, right?" you say.

You must also undergo the suffering of process. From a child you grow to be an adult; from adulthood you move onto old age. And you don't quite know how it happened. In thought after thought, there is change and decay. It never stops, like the waves on the sea. Moment by moment, day by day, month by month, year by year, the process continues. There's no way you can stop it. Birth, dwelling, change, and extinction continue ceaselessly. That's the suffering of process—the process of continual change. I can only speak of them in general. I'd never finish if I spoke of them in detail.

There are also eight kinds of sufferings:

1. Birth. When people are born, it's like ripping the shell from a live turtle. It hurts! That's why children cry when they are born; they know it's suffering.

2. Old age. Old people know what it's like. Young people have no way of knowing, and they don't understand when you try to tell them. Once they get old and their eyes, ears, and teeth all quit on them, their legs and hands go on

strike, then they know. Would you say that was suffering or not? You try to take a walk, and your legs won't move. You try to read something: "Hey, eyes, help me out here!" but your eyes say, "I'm too tired." Your ears fall in with your eyes and go deaf. Then your teeth fall out. Your hands shake, so you can't write. Would you say that was suffering or not? Why does that happen? Because you didn't cultivate. The suffering of old age is very democratic; everyone must undergo it.

3. Sickness. Sickness is also very democratic: Everyone gets sick, even the emperor. When the president gets sick, he has to go to the doctor or the hospital. You can be a king or a minister, or any other person of high position, but if you get sick you are going to suffer. Chinese people take herbal medicines, and that's bitter, too. Most people have experienced the suffering of sickness. What everyone hasn't yet experienced is the suffering of death.

4. Death. Death is like ripping the skin off a live cow: Do you think that hurts or not? It's just as painful when the time comes to die and the four elements return to their source. Can you imagine the cries of a cow if you tried to flay it alive? That's about how much it hurts to die.

5. The suffering of being separated from what you love. This is the fiercest of all. Say you love someone, and because of some special circumstance, that person has to leave you. Perhaps he goes into the army or off on business. Then you really suffer. It's painful but unavoidable.

6. The suffering of being joined with what you hate. You keep running into the very person you just can't stand. That's very painful, too.

7. The suffering of not getting what you want. You may

have hopes and wishes, but somehow you never fulfill them. This is the suffering of not getting what you want. A man might want to find a good wife, or a woman might want to find a good husband, but it's not easy. Perhaps you get to be thirty, forty, or fifty years old, and you still don't find anyone. What misery! Then you feel you have wasted your whole life. In general, not getting what you want is suffering.

"I'm not concerned with birth, old age, sickness, or death," you say, "and I don't love or hate anyone. I don't wish for anything. I don't suffer, do I?" you ask.

Hah! Who would have guessed that right within you, the five *skandhas* are raging. This is:

8. The suffering of the raging blaze of the five *skandhas*. Form, feeling, thinking, formations, and consciousness—the five *skandhas*—turn you upside down, and they rage incessantly like a huge conflagration.

Those are the eight sufferings. I would like to lecture them in more detail, but time is not polite, so I have just spoken in general terms.

The second of the Four Truths is accumulation. Accumulation refers to the amassing of afflictions. There are twenty kinds of subsidiary afflictions. There are great afflictions, middle-sized afflictions, and lesser afflictions.

The third of the Four Truths is extinction. Cultivating the Way is the cause of the extinction of all suffering, and extinction is the attainment of the wonderful fruition of Nirvana. And the fourth of the Four Truths is the Way, the path that must be cultivated. The Buddha spoke the Dharma of the Four Truths for the Hearers **to take them across birth, old age, sickness, and death to ultimate Nirvana**, so that they can ultimately attain the wonderful virtues of Nirvana: permanence, bliss, true self, and purity.

To those who sought to be Pratyekabuddhas, he spoke the Dharma of the Twelve Causes and Conditions. *Pratyekabuddha* means "enlightened by conditions." Pratyekabuddhas are of two kinds. When the Buddha is in the world, they cultivate the Twelve Causes and Conditions and thereby awaken to the Way. When there is no Buddha in the world, they cultivate by themselves and reach an awakening on their own, and so they are called Solitary Enlightened Ones.

The Twelve Causes and Conditions are:

1. Ignorance. Ignorance comes from lack of enlightenment. Once there is ignorance, then there is
2. Activity. Once there is activity then there is
3. Consciousness, the discriminating consciousness. Once there is consciousness then there is
4. Name and form. Once there is name and form, then there are
5. Six entrances—the eye, ear, nose, tongue, body, and mind. Once there are six entrances then there is
6. Contact. Once there is contact then there is
7. Feeling. With feeling there is
8. Love. Once there is love there is
9. Grasping. Grasping conditions
10. Becoming. Becoming conditions
11. Birth, which conditions
12. Old age and death.

The twelve links come into being in this way. If you reverse the list, you have their progression back into extinction:

1. When ignorance is extinguished,
2. Activity is extinguished. When activity is extinguished,
3. Consciousness is extinguished. When consciousness is extinguished,
4. Name and form are extinguished. When name and form are extinguished,
5. The six entrances are extinguished. When the six entrances are extinguished,
6. Contact is extinguished. When contact is extinguished,
7. Feeling is extinguished. When feeling is extinguished,
8. Love is extinguished. When love is extinguished,
9. Grasping is extinguished. When grasping is extinguished,
10. Becoming is extinguished. When becoming is extinguished,
11. Birth is extinguished. When birth is extinguished,
12. Old age and death are extinguished.

For the Bodhisattvas, in order to lead them to *anuttarasamyaksambodhi,* he spoke the Dharma of the Six Paramitas, which culminates in Buddha-wisdom. The Buddha King of Awesome Sound taught the Bodhisattvas about giving, morality, patience, vigor, *dhyana* samadhi, and wisdom. These six are the Bodhisattva Dharmas of cultivation; they are Dharmas for benefiting yourself and benefiting others, for enlightening yourself and enlightening others.

Why are they called *paramitas*? *Paramita* is a Sanskrit word, which means "arrived at the other shore." Cultivating any of these six, you can go from this shore, the shore of birth and death, through the flow of afflictions and arrive at the other shore of Nirvana. The cultivation of these leads to the ultimate wisdom of the Buddha.

Sutra:

"Great Strength, the Buddha King of Awesome Sound had a life span of eons equal in number to the grains of sand in forty myriads of *kotis* of *nayutas* of Ganges Rivers."

I5. The Buddha's life span.

Commentary:

Great Strength Bodhisattva, **the Buddha King of Awesome Sound had a life span of eons equal in number to the grains of sand in forty myriads of *kotis* of *nayutas* of Ganges Rivers**—that long a time.

Sutra:

"His proper Dharma dwelt in the world for eons equal in number to the motes of dust in a single Jambudvipa. The Dharma Image Age dwelt in the world for eons equal in number to the motes of dust in one set of four continents. After benefiting living beings, he passed into stillness."

I6. The Proper and Image Ages.

Commentary:

His proper Dharma dwelt in the world for eons equal in

number to the motes of dust in a single Jambudvipa. The Dharma Image Age dwelt in the world for eons equal in number to the motes of dust in one set of four continents. Jambudvipa is just one of the four continents. **After benefiting living beings, he passed into stillness.** After he had taught and transformed the living beings he was supposed to teach and transform, he then entered Nirvana.

Sutra:

> **"After the Proper and Image Dharma had become completely extinct, in this country yet another Buddha appeared, also by the name of King of Awesome Sound Thus Come One, One Worthy of Offerings, One of Proper and Pervasive Knowledge, One Perfect in Clarity and Conduct, Well Gone One, One Who Understands the World, Unsurpassed Lord, Regulating Hero, Teacher of Gods and Humans, Buddha, World Honored One. In this way, in sequence, there were twenty thousand *kotis* of Buddhas, all of the same name."**

H2. The twenty thousand *kotis* of successive Buddhas.

Commentary:

After the Proper and Image Dharma. When the Buddha is in the world, that is the time of the Proper Dharma. Once the Buddha enters Nirvana, that is called the Dharma Image Age. During such a time, the Buddhadharma and Buddha images still remain in the world. But after both the Proper Dharma Age and the Dharma Image Age **had become completely extinct, in this country** called Great Accomplishment **yet another Buddha appeared, also by the name**

of King of Awesome Sound Thus Come One, One Worthy of Offerings, One of Proper and Pervasive Knowledge, One Perfect in Clarity and Conduct, Well Gone One, One Who Understands the World, Unsurpassed Lord, Regulating Hero, Teacher of Gods and Humans, Buddha, World Honored One. In this way, in sequence, one after another, **there were twenty thousand *kotis* of Buddhas, all of the same name.** They were all called King of Awesome Sound Thus Come One.

Sutra:

> **"When the first Thus Come One King of Awesome Sound had passed into stillness, and after the extinction of his proper Dharma, during the Dharma Image Age there were Bhikshus of overweening pride who assumed great power. At that time there was a Bhikshu-Bodhisattva by the name of Never-Slighting."**

G2. Past affairs.
H1. The two names.

Commentary:

When the first Thus Come One King of Awesome Sound had passed into stillness, and after the extinction of his proper Dharma, during the Dharma Image Age there were Bhikshus of overweening pride who assumed great power. They thought they were higher and more important than anybody. Because of overweening pride they fought for name and profit, and they gained tremendous power and influence over Buddhism.

At that time, during the Dharma Image Age, **there was a**

Bhikshu-Bodhisattva by the name of Never-Slighting. He was a Bhikshu-Bodhisattva because he practiced the Bodhisattva Path.

Sutra:

> **"Great Strength, for what reason was he called Never-Slighting? Whomever this Bhikshu met, be it a Bhikshu, Bhikshuni, Upasaka, or Upasika, he would bow to them all and praise them, saying, 'I deeply respect all of you and dare not slight you. Why? You are all practicing the Bodhisattva Path and shall attain Buddhahood.'**
>
> **"This Bhikshu did not read and recite Sutras, but specialized in making obeisance to the point that when he saw the four assemblies from afar, he would approach them, bow, and praise them, saying, 'I dare not slight you, for you shall all become Buddhas.'"**

H2. Faith and slander.
I1. What faithful ones gained.

Commentary:

Great Strength, for what reason was he called Never-Slighting? Whomever this Bhikshu met, be it a Bhikshu, Bhikshuni, Upasaka, or Upasika, he would bow to them all and praise them. Now a Bhikshu does not ordinarily bow to a Bhikshuni or a layperson. But the Bodhisattva Never-Slighting did this because he wished to practice the Bodhisattva Path. Bodhisattvas have no mark of a self. They are of one substance with everyone else. They have no mark of a self, no mark of others, no mark of living beings, and no mark of a life span.

"If there is no mark of a self, others, living beings, or a life, why did he bow to the other Bhikshus, Bhikshunis, Upasakas, and Upasikas? Isn't bowing a kind of mark?" you ask.

His bowing was a "markless mark." Why? If he had had a mark, he wouldn't have been able to bow. Why didn't the Bhikshus of overweening pride practice bowing like this? They didn't cultivate this practice because they had a mark of self. The Bodhisattva Never-Slighting had no mark of self. He saw the self as empty, and so he bowed to the other Bhikshus, Bhikshunis, Upasakas and Upasikas. He had no self. Having no self, when he saw members of the four assemblies, he would bow and praise them, **saying, "I deeply respect all of you and dare not slight you. Why?** Because **you are all practicing the Bodhisattva Path."** All of you—Bhikshus, Bhikshunis, Upasakas, and Upasikas—are benefiting yourselves and benefiting others, **and shall attain Buddhahood.** Cultivating the Bodhisattva Path, you shall quickly become Buddhas."

This Bhikshu did not read and recite Sutras, but specialized in making obeisance to the four assemblies, **to the point that when he saw the four assemblies from afar, he would approach them, bow, and praise them, saying, "I dare not slight you, for you shall all become Buddhas."** Such a practice is not easy to do. Could you do it? That was cultivating what others cannot cultivate.

Sutra:

> **"Within the four assemblies, there were some who grew irate, those with impure minds who reviled him with foul mouths, saying, 'Where did this senseless Bhikshu come from, who says "I dare not slight you"**

and then gives us predictions, saying we shall become Buddhas? We don't need such false predictions!'

"In this way for many years he was scolded and reviled. But he never got angry. He always said, 'You shall become Buddhas.' When he said that, those people would beat him with sticks or throw stones at him. He would run off, stand at a distance, and shout out, 'I dare not slight you, for you shall all become Buddhas!' Because he always said that, the Bhikshus, Bhikshunis, Upasakas, and Upasikas of overweening pride gave him the name 'Never-Slighting.'"

I2. What slanderers lost.

Commentary:

Within the four assemblies there were some who grew irate, those with impure minds who reviled him with foul mouths. When Never-Slighting Bodhisattva bowed to them, they would kick him in the head. Why did they get angry? It was because their minds were impure. Their minds were filled with the three poisons of greed, hatred, and stupidity. They had taken too much poison, too many hallucinogenic drugs. They were confused and unclean. They were as if drunk. And so they only berated him, **saying, "Where did this senseless**, idiotic, dim-witted **Bhikshu come from?"** They would scold him and beat him when he bowed to them. Would you say the Bodhisattva Path is easy to practice? It certainly is not. The angry Bhikshus said to Never-Slighting, "Where do you come from? You have absolutely no conception of the Buddhist awesome manner. How can you do this? There are three hundred modes of propriety and three thousand modes of awesome comportment. You haven't a single one!"

"Who is this person **who says 'I dare not slight you' and then gives us predictions, saying we shall become Buddhas?** Do you think it's that simple? You're really stupid! **We don't need such false predictions.** The Buddha is the only person who can give predictions. You raving maniac! You are a mess!"

In this way for many years he was scolded and reviled. It wasn't an isolated incident, in other words. **But he never got angry**, and he didn't retreat. If you had a mark of self and someone humiliated you, you would be afraid to continue practicing the Bodhisattva Path. But **he always said, "You shall become Buddhas."**

When he said that, those people would beat him with sticks or throw stones at him. They would see him bow, and thinking him too stupid, they would grab a stick and hit him or throw a rock at his head. **He would run off, stand at a distance, and shout out, "I dare not slight you, for you shall all become Buddhas!"** Even though he had no mark of self, it still hurt when they hit him. He would bow hastily, run off, and shout, "I dare not slight you, for you shall all become Buddhas!" He was known as the village idiot. Everybody scolded him, "You're crazy! How disgusting!"

Because he always said that, the Bhikshus, Bhikshunis, Upasakas, and Upasikas of overweening pride gave him the name "Never-Slighting." So, take care that you do not become a Bhikshu, Bhikshuni, Upasaka, or Upasika of overweening pride. It's not a game.

He didn't have this name to begin with, but because he

was always saying, "I dare not slight you," the ones of overweening pride nicknamed him "Never-Slighting."

Sutra:

"When this Bhikshu's life was coming to an end, in space he heard all of the complete twenty thousand myriad *kotis* of verses of the *Dharma Flower Sutra* previously spoken by the Buddha King of Awesome Sound. He was able to receive and uphold them all. He immediately obtained the purity of the eye and the purity of the ear, nose, tongue, body, and mind, as mentioned above. Having obtained the purity of the six senses, his life span was further increased by two million *kotis* of *nayutas* of years. He extensively spoke the *Dharma Flower Sutra* for others.

"At that time the four assemblies of Bhikshus, Bhikshunis, Upasakas, and Upasikas of overweening pride who had ridiculed him and named him Never-Slighting saw that he had gained great powers of spiritual penetrations, the power of the eloquence of delight in speech, and the power of great wholesome silence. Hearing what he said, they faithfully submitted to him and followed him. This Bodhisattva further transformed thousands of myriads of *kotis* of multitudes, causing them to dwell in *anuttarasamyaksambodhi*. When his life was over, he was able to encounter two thousand *kotis* of Buddhas, all named Brightness of Sun-Moon-Lamp. Within their Dharmas, he spoke the *Dharma Flower Sutra*. By means of these causes and conditions, he further encountered two

thousand *kotis* of Buddhas, all named Cloud-like Comfort Lamp King. Within the Dharma of those Buddhas, he received, upheld, read, recited, and spoke for others of the four assemblies this Sutra, and so obtained the purity of his ordinary eye and the purity of his ear, nose, tongue, body, and mind. He spoke the Dharma in the four assemblies with a heart free of fear.

"Great Strength, the Bodhisattva Mahasattva Never-Slighting made offerings to as many Buddhas as these: revering, honoring, and praising them and planting the roots of goodness.

"He later encountered a thousand myriad *kotis* of Buddhas, and within the Dharma of all these Buddhas, he spoke this Sutra. When his merit and virtue were realized, he became a Buddha."

H3. The results of faith and slander.
I1. The rewards of the faithful.
J1. The reward.

Commentary:

When this Bhikshu's life was coming to an end, when he was about to die, **in space he heard all of the complete twenty thousand myriad *kotis* of verses of the *Dharma Flower Sutra* previously spoken by the Buddha King of Awesome Sound. He was able to receive and uphold them all.** He could receive them with his mind and uphold them with his body. **He immediately obtained the purity of the eye and the purity of the ear, nose, tongue, body, and mind, as mentioned above,** as elucidated in the previous chapter, "The Merit and Virtue of a Dharma Master."

Having obtained the purity of the six senses, he did not die, but **his life span was further increased by two million *kotis* of *nayutas* of years. He extensively spoke the *Dharma Flower Sutra* for others.** He always lectured on the *Dharma Flower Sutra*.

The Bodhisattva Never-Slighting had just attained the purity of the six sense faculties. Although he had not been certified to the fruition, he had obtained these advantages with the body born of his parents, and he was always lecturing the *Dharma Flower Sutra* to others. **At that time the four assemblies of Bhikshus, Bhikshunis, Upasakas, and Upasikas of overweening pride who had ridiculed him and named him Never-Slighting saw that he had gained great powers of spiritual penetrations.** He was able to recite all the many verses of the *Dharma Flower Sutra*, and with his powerful wisdom and spiritual penetrations, lecture them to others. He had also gained **the power of the eloquence of delight in speech** in speaking Dharma **and the power of great wholesome silence.** When people scolded him, he did not get angry. Outwardly he displayed no distress, and inwardly he was not resentful. "Silence" means that he was able to bear the most unendurable things. That's because he had attained the power of patience and the power of *prajna* wisdom.

Hearing what he said, they faithfully submitted to him and followed him. Hearing him speak the *Dharma Flower Sutra*, they believed it, and they were tamed. They weren't like they had been before when they scolded and beat him. They followed him wherever he went to speak the Dharma.

This Bodhisattva further transformed thousands of myriads of *kotis* of multitudes, causing them to dwell in

anuttarasamyaksambodhi. He taught and transformed limitless, boundless living beings.

When his life was over, he was able to encounter two thousand *kotis* of Buddhas, all named Brightness of Sun-Moon-Lamp. After that life was over, in his next life he got to meet two thousand *kotis* of Buddhas. **Within their Dharmas, he spoke the *Dharma Flower Sutra*. By means of these causes and conditions**, because he spoke the *Dharma Flower Sutra*, **he further encountered two thousand *kotis* of Buddhas, all named Cloud-like Comfort Lamp King. Within the Dharma of those Buddhas, he received, upheld, read, recited, and spoke for others of the four assemblies this Sutra.** In life after life, Never-Slighting Bodhisattva spoke the *Dharma Flower Sutra*.

And so obtained the purity of his ordinary eye and was able to see throughout the three thousand great thousand world system. **And** he also obtained **the purity of his ear, nose, tongue, body, and mind. He spoke the Dharma in the four assemblies with a heart free of fear.**

Great Strength, the Bodhisattva Mahasattva Never-Slighting, who never looked down on living beings, **made offerings to as many Buddhas as these: revering, honoring, and praising them and planting the roots of goodness** in the presence of those Buddhas.

He later encountered a thousand myriad *kotis* of Buddhas, and within the Dharma of all these Buddhas, he spoke this Sutra. When his merit and virtue were realized, he became a Buddha. He himself realized Buddhahood.

Sutra:

"Great Strength, what do you think? At that time,

could the Bodhisattva Never-Slighting have been anyone else? He was none other than myself! Had I not in former lives received, upheld, read, and recited this Sutra and explained it to others, I would not have been able to gain *anuttarasamyaksambodhi* so quickly. Because in the presence of former Buddhas I received, upheld, read, and recited this Sutra and explained it to others, I quickly gained *anuttarasamyaksambodhi*."

J2. Conclusion—the past and present.

Commentary:

Shakyamuni Buddha calls out, **"Great Strength, what do you think? At that time, could the Bodhisattva Never-Slighting have been anyone else? He was none other than myself,** when I was practicing the Bodhisattva Path as a Bodhisattva. **Had I not in former lives received, upheld, read, and recited this Sutra and explained it to others, I would not have been able to gain *anuttarasamyaksambodhi***—the utmost, proper and equal, right enlightenment—**so quickly. Because in the presence of former Buddhas I received, upheld, read, and recited this Sutra and explained it to others, I quickly gained *anuttarasamyaksambodhi*."**

Sutra:

"Great Strength, because at that time the four assemblies of Bhikshus, Bhikshunis, Upasakas, and Upasikas hatefully reviled me, for two hundred *kotis*

of eons they did not encounter a Buddha or hear the Dharma or meet the Sangha. For a thousand eons they suffered great torment in the Avici Hell. Having received their punishment, they once again encountered Never-Slighting Bodhisattva, who taught and transformed them to *anuttarasamyaksambodhi*."

I2. The retribution for slanderers.
J1. The retribution.

Commentary:

Great Strength, because at that time the four assemblies of Bhikshus, Bhikshunis, Upasakas, and Upasikas hatefully reviled me and looked down on me, saying that I was a dumb Bhikshu, **for two hundred *kotis* of eons they did not encounter a Buddha.** Now that we have come upon the Buddhadharma, we know that we're not without good roots. People without good roots have no way to hear even the name of the Buddha **or hear the Dharma or meet the Sangha**—or even see a Bhikshu or Bhikshuni. Now in this country the Sangha has appeared. One must have good roots to meet with the Triple Jewel. Because those of overweening pride slighted and scolded Never-Slighting Bodhisattva, for two hundred *kotis* of eons they didn't hear the name of the Triple Jewel. **For a thousand eons they suffered great torment in the Avici Hell. Having received their punishment,** they again got to be human beings, and **they once again encountered Never-Slighting Bodhisattva, who taught and transformed them to *anuttarasamyaksambodhi*.** He taught them and caused them to bring forth the mind for the utmost, proper and equal, right enlightenment.

Sutra:

"Great Strength, what do you think? At that time could the four assemblies who constantly slighted this Bodhisattva have been anyone else? They were just Bhadrapala Bodhisattva and the five hundred Bodhisattvas in this assembly, Lion Moon and the five hundred Bhikshus, and Sugatachetana and the five hundred Upasakas, all of whom are irreversible from *anuttarasamyaksambodhi*."

J2. The conclusion—past and present.

Commentary:

Great Strength, what do you think? At that time could the four assemblies who constantly slighted this Bodhisattva have been anyone else? They were just Bhadrapala Bodhisattva and the five hundred Bodhisattvas in this assembly. "Bhadrapala" means "good protection." In the past he slighted the Bodhisattva, but having been taught and transformed by him, he is now one of his good protectors, and he conscientiously follows the rules as well. That assembly in the past also included **Lion Moon and the five hundred Bhikshus**—he spoke the Dharma like a lion and his wisdom was as bright as the moon. **And Sugatachetana and the five hundred Upasakas, all of whom are irreversible from *anuttarasamyaksambodhi*** were there. They have cultivated the Way to the level of nonretreat. They won't fall back again.

Sutra:

"Great Strength, you should know that the *Dharma*

Flower Sutra **greatly benefits all the Bodhisattvas Mahasattvas, causing them to arrive at *anuttara-samyaksambodhi*. Therefore, after the passing into stillness of the Thus Come One all the Bodhisattvas Mahasattvas should always receive, uphold, read, and recite this Sutra, explain it to others, and write it out."**

F3. Exhortation to uphold.

Commentary:

Great Strength, you should know that the *Dharma Flower Sutra* greatly benefits all the Bodhisattvas Mahasattvas, causing them to arrive at *anuttarasamyaksambodhi*—the utmost, right and equal, proper enlightenment. **Therefore, after the passing into stillness of the Thus Come One,** Shakyamuni Buddha, **all the Bodhisattvas Mahasattvas should always receive, uphold, read, and recite this Sutra, explain it to others, and write it out.** According to how much merit and virtue you create, you will receive that much in the way of advantages. There is nothing false about this at all.

When people listen to Sutras, the more they hear, the better they should like it. The better they like it, the more they should listen. Studying the Buddhadharma should be even more delightful than eating honey. The Buddhadharma is sweet dew. Sweet dew is the medicine of immortality. Hearing the Buddhadharma, you can start out confused and then wake up. Not understanding, you can gain understanding. Why did the Buddha speak the Dharma? So that living beings could understand it. The Buddhadharma isn't that easy to understand either. It's difficult to understand because it's too wonderful; it's inconceivable. Although it's not easy to understand, we should be determined to find a way to understand it. You can't say that because it's difficult to understand, you won't study. The more you don't understand, the more you should study. When you have attained the fourth stage of Arhatship, you will reach the stage beyond study. Although we say it's the stage beyond study, it applies only to the fruit of the Small Vehicle. According to the Great Vehicle, there is still studying to do, because this position is not ultimate. One still has to study the practice of the Bodhisattva and the Six Perfections and the Ten Thousand Conducts. Therefore, those who haven't been certified to the fourth fruit of Arhatship need to study. If you don't understand, you've got to study. If you do understand, you should study even more.

"If I understand, then why do I need to study?" you ask.

Because there are still things which you don't understand. If you have completely understood the *Dharma Flower Sutra*, you still haven't mastered the *Shurangama Sutra*. If you have mastered the entire *Shurangama Sutra*, then there is the *Avatamsaka Sutra*. And so the Buddhadharma is like the great sea. Living beings float in the great sea of the Buddhadharma. How should we study it? You can start with the Six Paramitas. First, learn about giving. "Giving" doesn't mean that you tell others to give to you; it means that you give to others. So practice giving. Second, learn how to keep the precepts. Third, develop your patience. The fourth paramita is vigor, the fifth is *dhyana* samadhi, and the sixth is *prajna* wisdom.

Sutra:

At that time the World Honored One, wishing to restate this meaning, spoke verses, saying,

In the past there was a Buddha
By the name of King of Awesome Sound.
With limitless spiritual powers and wisdom,
He guided all living beings.
Gods, humans, dragons, and spirits
Made offerings to him.

E2. Verse.
F1. Rewards and retribution for faith and slander.
G1. The origins.

Commentary:

At that time the World Honored One, Shakyamuni Buddha, **wishing to restate this meaning, spoke verses, saying, *"In the past there was a Buddha / By the name of King of Awesome Sound. / With limitless spiritual powers and wisdom, / He guided all living beings."*** He led all living beings to bring forth the resolve for Bodhi and to quickly realize the Buddha Way. ***Gods, humans, dragons, and spirits / Made offerings to him.*** The gods, dragons, and eightfold division all made offerings to him.

Sutra:

After this Buddha's passing into stillness,
When the Dharma was about to become extinct,
There was a Bodhisattva

By the name of Never-Slighting.
At that time the four assemblies were
attached to the Dharma.

G2. Past affairs.
H1. The two names.

Commentary:

After this Buddha's passing into stillness, / When the Dharma was about to become extinct. This Buddha propagated the Dharma in the world for a long time. Then he entered Nirvana. After the Proper Dharma Age and the Dharma Image Age had transpired, ***there was a Bodhisattva / By the name of Never-Slighting.*** He treated all living beings as respectfully as one would the Buddha. ***At that time the four assemblies*** had heavy karmic obstacles. That being the Dharma Ending Age, they didn't cultivate. They were called left-home people, but they didn't really cultivate. They were arrogant and haughty; they thought of themselves as better than everyone else. "I alone am honored!" was their pet saying. When Shakyamuni Buddha was born, he pointed one finger to the heavens and one to the earth, and said, "In the heavens and below, I alone am honored." The Buddha can say things like that, but ordinary people cannot. This is like those externalists who say, "I am the Buddha. You should make offerings to me."

They ***were attached to the Dharma.*** Basically, even the Dharma has to be relinquished, how much the more so that which is not Dharma. If you don't understand the Dharma, you must study it. Once you understand it, you have to put it down. You can't cling to the Dharma. At that time, because the Buddhadharma was about to become extinct, the Bhikshus, Bhikshunis, Upasakas, and Upasikas were all attached to the superficial aspects of the Dharma. Not only did they fail to understand the Dharma, but they were attached to it. Attached to the Dharma, they gave rise to overweening pride.

Sutra:

> ***The Bodhisattva Never-Slighting***
> ***Would approach them***
> ***And say to them,***
> ***"I will not slight you,***
> ***For you are practicing the Way***
> ***And shall become Buddhas."***
> ***Hearing that, they slighted him,***
> ***Slandered and reviled him,***
> ***And Never-Slighting Bodhisattva***
> ***endured it all.***

H2. Faith and slander.

Commentary:

The Bodhisattva Never-Slighting / Would approach them—the Bhikshus of overweening pride—***and say to them, / "I will not slight you, / For you are practicing the Way,*** the Bodhisattva Path, ***and shall become Buddhas."*** In the future you will all become Buddhas.

Hearing that, they slighted him. Those so attached to the Dharma ***slandered and reviled him, / And Never-Slighting Bodhisattva endured it all.*** People yelled at him, hit him with sticks, and threw rocks at him. Never-Slighting

Bodhisattva didn't get angry in the least. No matter how cruel people were to him, he was patient.

Sutra:

> ***When his punishment was finished,***
> ***At the end of his life,***
> ***He got to hear this Sutra,***
> ***And his six sense faculties were purified.***
> ***By the power of spiritual penetrations,***
> ***His life span was increased,***
> ***And for the sake of others,***
> ***He vastly spoke this Sutra.***
> ***The multitudes who were attached to***
> ***Dharma***
> ***All received this Bodhisattva's***
> ***Teaching and successfully***
> ***Were led to dwell in the Buddha Way.***
> ***When Never-Slighting's life ended,***
> ***He met with countless Buddhas,***
> ***And because he spoke this Sutra,***
> ***He obtained limitless blessings.***
> ***Gradually perfecting his merit and virtue,***
> ***He quickly realized the Buddha Way.***
> ***At that time Never-Slighting***
> ***Was indeed myself!***

H3. Rewards and retributions.
I1. Rewards of the faithful.

Commentary:

When his punishment was finished, Never-Slighting Bodhisattva bowed to everyone. Why did he have offenses? They weren't from bowing; they were offenses from former lives that he had not yet paid for. The *Vajra Sutra* says, "Moreover, Subhuti, if a good man or good woman receives, holds, reads, and recites this Sutra and if people ridicule him, that person has karmic offenses from previous lives which destine him for the evil paths. But because in his present life he is ridiculed by others, his previous karmic offenses are destroyed, and he will attain *anuttarasamyaksambodhi.*"

Never-Slighting Bodhisattva practiced never ridiculing people. He was scolded, hit, and maligned by others, and so the offenses he had incurred from having ridiculed others in former lives were canceled out. Since they were all gone, ***at the end of his life, / He got to hear this Sutra***—the *Dharma Flower Sutra* and this inconceivable doctrine—***and his six sense faculties were purified. / By the power of spiritual penetrations, / His life span was increased.*** With his great powers not only did he not die, but he increased his life span. ***And for the sake of others, he vastly spoke this Sutra,*** expounding upon it. ***The multitudes who were attached to Dharma***—the Bhikshus, Bhikshunis, Upasakas, and Upasikas of overweening pride who were attached to the Dharma and fell into the hells—after they had received their punishment, were reborn again as people. Seeing the awesome spiritual powers Never-Slighting Bodhisattva had attained, the great power of wholesome silence, ***all received this Bodhisattva's / Teaching and successfully / Were led to dwell in the Buddha Way.***

When Never-Slighting's life ended, / He met with countless Buddhas. Life after life, he met with countless Buddhas,

and because he constantly ***spoke this Sutra, / He obtained limitless blessings. / Gradually perfecting his merit and virtue*** of the Bodhisattva Path, ***he quickly realized the Buddha Way. / At that time Never-Slighting / Was indeed myself!*** It was I, Shakyamuni Buddha in a former life when I was practicing the Bodhisattva Path of universal respect.

Sutra:

> ***At that time the four assemblies***
> ***Were attached to the Dharma.***
> ***Hearing Never-Slighting's words,***
> ***"You shall become Buddhas,"***
> ***By means of those causes and conditions***
> ***Were countless Buddhas encountered.***
> ***The multitude of five hundred***
> ***Bodhisattvas in this assembly***
> ***And the men and women of pure faith***
> ***Within the four assemblies***
> ***Are now in front of me,***
> ***Listening to the Dharma.***
> ***In former lives***
> ***I exhorted these people***
> ***To listen to and receive this Sutra,***
> ***Which is the foremost Dharma.***
> ***I instructed them***
> ***And led them to dwell in Nirvana,***
> ***And life after life, to receive and uphold***
> ***A Sutra such as this.***

I2. Retribution for slanderers.

Commentary:

At that time the four assemblies / Were attached to the Dharma. / Hearing Never-Slighting's words, / "You shall become Buddhas," / By means of those causes and conditions, / Were countless Buddhas encountered. / The multitude of five hundred / Bodhisattvas in this assembly. Bhadrapala Bodhisattva and those Bhikshus and Bhikshunis of overweening pride have now attained irreversibility. Now they keep the precepts very well, but long ago they slandered the Bodhisattva Never-Slighting. ***And the men and women of pure faith / Within the four assemblies / Are now in front of me.*** They are all right here. In the past they ridiculed, slighted, and slandered me. Now they have all brought forth the Bodhi mind. Why have they brought forth the Bodhi mind? Because I planted the Bodhi seed in them by saying, "I dare not slight you, for you shall all become Buddhas." I gave them predictions and also bowed to them. Because of this, they are now ***listening to the Dharma.*** They are right here listening to me speak the *Dharma Flower Sutra*. It wasn't always like this, however.

In former lives / I exhorted these people / To listen to and receive this Sutra, to bring forth the Bodhi mind and cultivate the Bodhisattva Path. I always lectured upon the *Dharma Flower Sutra* and they listened to it. ***Which is the foremost Dharma.*** The *Dharma Flower Sutra* is number one, the most wonderful of Buddhadharmas. ***I instructed them / And led them to dwell in Nirvana*** to obtain the happiness of Nirvana with its four virtues of permanence, bliss, true self, and purity. ***And life after life, to receive and uphold / A Sutra such as this.*** I taught and transformed these living beings, life after life. They received and upheld the *Dharma Flower Sutra*. I myself also received and upheld it, life after life.

Sutra:

> ***For only in millions and millions***
> ***of myriads of eons,***
> ***Inconceivable in number,***
> ***Can one get to hear***
> ***The* Dharma Flower Sutra.**
> ***And only in millions and millions***
> ***of myriads of eons,***
> ***Inconceivable in number,***
> ***Do the Buddhas, World Honored Ones,***
> ***Happen to speak this Sutra.***
> ***Therefore, the practitioner,***
> ***After the Buddha's passing,***
> ***On hearing this Sutra,***
> ***Should not give rise to doubts,***
> ***But should, with a single mind,***
> ***Extensively proclaim this Sutra,***
> ***So that life after life he may meet***
> ***the Buddhas***
> ***And quickly realize the Buddha Way.***

F2. Exhortation to uphold.

Commentary:

For only in millions and millions of myriads of eons, / Inconceivable in number, / Can one get to hear / The* Dharma Flower Sutra.** In limitless eons one may not get to hear it. It is difficult to encounter. ***And only in millions and millions of myriads of eons, / Inconceivable in number, / Do the Buddhas, World Honored Ones, / Happen to speak this Sutra.

Therefore, the practitioner, you who cultivate the Bodhisattva Path, ***after the Buddha's passing, / On hearing this Sutra, / Should not give rise to doubts.*** He shouldn't have doubts, ***but should, with a single mind, / Extensively proclaim this Sutra*** for everyone, ***so that life after life he may meet the Buddhas / And quickly realize the Buddha Way.*** Now that you have heard the *Dharma Flower Sutra,* you should lecture on it wherever you go.

End of Chapter Twenty

The Buddhas, ones who save the world,
Dwelling in great spiritual penetrations,
In order to delight living beings,
Manifest limitless spiritual powers.
Their tongues reach to the Brahma Heavens,
Their bodies emit countless lights.
They make appear these rare events,
For the sake of those who seek the Buddha Way.

The Wonderful Dharma Lotus Flower Sutra

Chapter Twenty-one: The Spiritual Powers of the Thus Come One

Sutra:

AT THAT TIME THE Bodhisattvas Mahasattvas equal in number to the motes of dust in a thousand worlds, who had welled forth out of the earth, in the presence of the Buddha, single-mindedly, with palms joined, gazed up at the Buddha and spoke to him, saying, "World Honored One, after the Buddha's passing, in countries where there are division bodies of the Buddha, in places where he has passed into stillness, we shall extensively speak this Sutra. Why? Because we also wish to obtain this true, pure, and great Dharma; to receive, uphold, read and recite, explain, write out, and make offerings to it."

At that time, in the presence of Manjushri and the others, limitless hundreds of thousands of myriads of *kotis* of Bodhisattvas Mahasattvas who had long resided in the Saha world, as well as the Bhikshus, Bhikshunis,

Upasakas, Upasikas, gods, dragons, *yakshas, gandharvas, asuras, garudas, kinnaras, mahoragas,* humans, non-humans, and so forth, the World Honored One manifested great spiritual powers.

He put forth his vast and long tongue which reached upward to the Brahma worlds. From all of his hair pores, he emitted lights of limitless, countless colors, all of which pervasively illuminated the worlds of the ten directions. In the same way, all the Buddhas seated on lion thrones beneath jeweled trees also put forth their vast and long tongues and emitted limitless lights.

When Shakyamuni Buddha and the Buddhas beneath the jeweled trees had manifested their spiritual powers for a full hundred thousand years, they withdrew their tongues.

Then they coughed and snapped their fingers, and those two sounds pervaded the Buddha worlds of the ten directions.

The earth quaked in six ways and the living beings in those worlds—the gods, dragons, *yakshas, gandharvas, asuras, garudas, kinnaras, mahoragas,* humans, non-humans, and so forth—by means of the Buddha's spiritual powers, all saw, in the Saha world, the limitless, boundless, hundreds of thousands of myriads of *kotis* of Buddhas seated on lion thrones beneath jeweled trees. They also saw Shakyamuni Buddha, together with the Thus Come One Many Jewels, seated on the lion throne within the jeweled stupa.

They further saw limitless, boundless, hundreds of thousands of myriads of *kotis* of Bodhisattvas Mahasattvas, as well as the four assemblies, reverently circumambulating Shakyamuni Buddha. Having seen this, they

they greatly rejoiced, having gained what they had never had.

Just then the gods in space called out in a loud voice: "Passing from here through limitless, boundless, hundreds of thousands of myriads of *kotis* of *asamkhyeyas* of worlds, there is a country called Saha. Within it is a Buddha named Shakyamuni who now, for the sake of all the Bodhisattvas Mahasattvas, proclaims a Great Vehicle Sutra by the name of the *Wonderful Dharma Lotus Flower*, a Dharma for teaching Bodhisattvas, of whom the Buddha is protective and mindful. You should all rejoice deep within your hearts, bow, and make offerings to Shakyamuni Buddha."

Hearing this sound in space, all the living beings placed their palms together, faced the Saha world, and said, "Namo Shakyamuni Buddha! Namo Shakyamuni Buddha!"

And then from afar, they scattered all kinds of flowers, incense, beads, banners, canopies, ornaments for the body, and precious and rare objects on the Saha world. The objects they scattered came from the ten directions like clouds gathering, and turned into jeweled canopies, completely covering the Buddhas in that region.

Then the worlds of the ten directions interpenetrated without obstruction, as if they were one Buddhaland.

At that time the Buddha told Superior Conduct and all the great assembly of Bodhisattvas, "The spiritual power of all the Buddhas is limitless, boundless, and inconceivable like this. If, using these spiritual powers, I were to speak of the meritorious virtues of this Sutra for limitless, boundless, hundreds of thousands of myriads of *kotis* of *asamkhyeyas* of eons by way of entrustment, I could not finish.

"In general, all the Dharmas of the Thus Come One, all the sovereign spiritual powers of the Thus Come One, all the secret storehouses of the Thus Come One, all the extremely profound deeds of the Thus Come One are all proclaimed and revealed in this Sutra.

"Therefore, all of you, after the passing of the Thus Come One, should with a single mind receive, uphold, read, recite, and explain it, write it out, and cultivate it as spoken. Those who receive, uphold, read, recite, explain, write out, and cultivate it as spoken, in whatever land they may be, in a place where the Sutra is kept: whether in a garden, in a forest, or beneath a tree; in a Sangha dwelling; in the dwelling of the white-robed; in a palace or hall; or in the mountains, valleys, or wilderness—in all of these places they should build a *stupa* and make offerings.

"For what reason? You should know that this place is a Way-place wherein all Buddhas gain *anuttarasamyak-sambodhi,* wherein all Buddhas turn the Dharma-wheel, and wherein all Buddhas enter Nirvana."

At that time the World Honored One, wishing to restate this meaning, spoke verses, saying,

The Buddhas, ones who save the world,
Dwelling in great spiritual penetrations,
In order to delight living beings,
Manifest limitless spiritual powers.
Their tongues reach to the Brahma Heavens,
Their bodies emit countless lights.
They make appear these rare events

For the sake of those who seek the Buddha Way.
The sounds made when the Buddhas cough
And the sounds made when they snap their fingers
Are heard throughout the lands of the ten directions
As the earth quakes in six ways.
Since after the Buddha's passing
One can uphold this Sutra,
All Buddhas rejoice
And display limitless spiritual powers.
In order to bequeath this Sutra,
He praises those who receive and hold it.
Doing so throughout limitless eons,
Still he cannot finish.
The merit and virtue of these people
Is boundless and infinite,
Like space in the ten directions,
Without any boundary.
Those who can uphold this Sutra
Have already seen me
And also seen the Buddha Many Jewels
And all of the division bodies.
They also see me on this day
Teaching and transforming the Bodhisattvas.
Those who can uphold this Sutra
Cause me and my division bodies
And the previous Buddha, Many Jewels,
To all rejoice.
They shall also see and make offerings
To the Buddhas of the ten directions—
in the present,
The past, and the future—

Causing them to rejoice as well.
The secret and essential Dharma obtained
By the Buddhas seated in their Way-places
Will also be gained before too long
By those who can uphold this Sutra.
Those who can uphold this Sutra
Will take delight in speaking, without end,
The meaning of the Dharmas,
Their names and expressions,
Like the wind blowing through space,
Without obstacle.
After the Thus Come One's passing,
They will understand the Sutras spoken
by the Buddha,
The causes and conditions in sequence,
And speak them truly, according with
their meanings.
Like the light of the sun and moon
Dispelling all darkness,
These people walk through the world
Dispersing the darkness of living beings,
Teaching limitless Bodhisattvas
Ultimately to dwell in the One Vehicle.
Therefore, those with wisdom,
Hearing the advantages of this merit
and virtue,
Should, after my passing,
Receive and uphold this Sutra.
These people most certainly and
without a doubt
Will attain the Buddha Way.

Chapter Twenty-one: The Spiritual Powers of the Thus Come One

A Simple Explanation by the Venerable Master Hsuan Hua

Sutra:

AT THAT TIME the Bodhisattvas Mahasattvas equal in number to the motes of dust in a thousand worlds, who had welled forth out of the earth, in the presence of the Buddha, single-mindedly, with palms joined, gazed up at the Buddha and spoke to him, saying, "World Honored One, after the Buddha's passing, in countries where there are division bodies of the Buddha, in places where he has passed into stillness, we shall extensively speak this Sutra. Why? Because we also wish to obtain this true, pure, and great Dharma; to receive, uphold, read and recite, explain, write out, and make offerings to it."

A3. Propagation—roots and traces.
B1. Bequeathing the job of propagation—Chapters on "Spiritual Powers" and "The Entrustment"
C1. Chapter on "Spiritual Powers"—Bodhisattvas receive a command to propagate the Sutra.

D1. Prose.
E1. Bodhisattvas receive the command.

Commentary:

This chapter is called **The Spiritual Powers of the Thus Come One.** "Thus Come One" is one of the Buddha's ten titles. "Thus" is stillness. "Come" is movement. "Thus" means "still and silent." "Come" means "able to be humane"—able to do the kind and humane work of the Buddha. "Still and silent" represents the comfortable spiritual powers enabling one to become a Buddha.

"Spiritual" means natural, not artificial. "Spiritual" refers to an inner quality. "Power" refers to external function. When there is internal spirituality, there is power outwardly. If you have no spirituality, there can be no power. "The spiritual powers of the Thus Come One" refers to the inconceivable, wonderful functioning of the Buddha's spiritual powers, an inconceivable state.

Even though we have discussed it at length, some people still don't understand the concept of spiritual power. I will now speak of it in general terms. It's like the previous appearance of Shakyamuni Buddha's division bodies of the ten directions. Where did they come from? They came from the spiritual power of Shakyamuni Buddha.

The Thus Come One Many Jewels came to the Way-place to certify the *Dharma Flower Sutra,* and this event also occurred through the spiritual power of the Thus Come One. The Bodhisattvas who welled forth out of the earth also did so through the spiritual power of the Thus Come One. The interpenetration of the six sense organs in the chapter "The Merit and Virtue of a Dharma Master" also happened through the spiritual power of the Thus Come One. Thus, the spiritual power of the Thus Come One is limitless and boundless. If you speak of it in detail, everything is a creation of the spiritual power of the Thus Come One.

At that time, when the chapter "Never-Slighting Bodhisattva" was finished, **the Bodhisattvas Mahasattvas** in the Dharma Flower Assembly **equal in number to the motes of dust in a thousand worlds, who had welled forth out of the earth**—these were all Bodhisattvas whom the Buddha in former lives had taught and transformed—**in the presence of the Buddha, single-mindedly, with palms joined,** reverent in body, **gazed up at the Buddha** with his fine marks **and spoke to him, saying, "World Honored One, after the Buddha's passing, in countries where there are division bodies of the Buddha, in places where he has passed into stillness,** regardless of which world or which country, wherever the World Honored One has manifested a division-body Buddha and then entered Nirvana, **we shall extensively speak this Sutra.** We will propagate the *Dharma Flower Sutra*. **Why? Because we also wish to obtain this true, pure, and great Dharma."** Bodhisattvas also wish to obtain this true, pure, and great Dharma. "True" represents the real Dharma. "Pure" represents the provisional Dharma. The real and the provisional are nondual—this is the great Dharma. The provisional is the real and the real is the provisional. This is the great Dharma of the nonduality of the provisional and the real.

"We wish **to receive, uphold, read and recite, explain, write out, and make offerings to it,** to the *Dharma Flower Sutra*."

Sutra:

At that time, in the presence of Manjushri and the others, limitless hundreds of thousands of myriads of *kotis* of Bodhisattvas Mahasattvas who had long resided in the Saha world, as well as the Bhikshus, Bhikshunis, Upasakas, Upasikas, gods, dragons, *yakshas, gandharvas, asuras, garudas, kinnaras, mahoragas,* humans, nonhumans, and so forth, the World Honored One manifested great spiritual powers.

E2. The Buddha manifests spiritual powers.
F1. The audience.

Commentary:

At that time, in the presence of Manjushri, Wonderfully Auspicious Bodhisattva, **and the others, limitless hundreds of thousands of myriads of *kotis* of Bodhisattvas Mahasattvas who had long resided in the Saha world**—these were Shakyamuni Buddha's old disciples, the great Bodhisattvas—**as well as the Bhikshus; Bhikshunis; Upasakas; Upasikas; gods; dragons; *yakshas; gandharvas,*** musical spirits; ***asuras,*** the ugly ones; ***garudas,*** the great golden-winged *peng* birds; ***kinnaras,*** also musical spirits; ***mahoragas,*** big snakes; **humans; nonhumans; and so forth, the World Honored One manifested great spiritual powers.**

Sutra:

He put forth his vast and long tongue which reached upward to the Brahma worlds. From all of his hair pores, he emitted lights of limitless, countless colors, all of which pervasively illuminated the worlds of the

ten directions. In the same way, all the Buddhas seated on lion thrones beneath jeweled trees also put forth their vast and long tongues and emitted limitless lights.

When Shakyamuni Buddha and the Buddhas beneath the jeweled trees had manifested their spiritual powers for a full hundred thousand years, they withdrew their tongues.

F2. The manifestation.
G1. Putting forth their tongues.
G2. Emitting light from their hair pores.

Commentary:

He put forth his vast and long tongue, which reached upward to the Brahma worlds. The Buddha's tongue reaches all the way up to his hairline. People with great blessings and virtue can touch their nose with their tongue. The tongue of the Perfect, Full Reward Body Buddha reaches all the way up to the Brahma Heaven. Here the Buddha is manifesting his great spiritual powers and putting forth his vast and long tongue. **From all of his hair pores, he emitted lights of limitless, countless colors, all of which pervasively illuminated the worlds of the ten directions.**

In the same way, all the Buddhas seated on lion thrones beneath jeweled trees also put forth their vast and long tongues and, like Shakyamuni Buddha, **emitted limitless lights** which shone upon the worlds of the ten directions.

When Shakyamuni Buddha and the Buddhas beneath the jeweled trees, the division body Buddhas, **had manifested their spiritual powers for a full hundred thousand years, they withdrew their tongues.**

Sutra:

Then they coughed and snapped their fingers, and those two sounds pervaded the Buddha worlds of the ten directions.

G3. Coughing.
G4. Snapping their fingers.

Commentary:

Then they coughed, very softly, to show they were thinking of living beings, to let them know they were there. This represents calling out and getting living beings' attention. The Buddhas of the ten directions all made this coughing sound at the same time.

And they then **snapped their fingers**; this represents alerting beings with sound. **And those two sounds pervaded the Buddha worlds of the ten directions.**

Sutra:

The earth quaked in six ways and the living beings in those worlds—the gods, dragons, *yakshas, gandharvas, asuras, garudas, kinnaras, mahoragas,* humans, non-humans, and so forth—by means of the Buddha's spiritual powers, all saw, in the Saha world, the limitless, boundless, hundreds of thousands of myriads of *kotis* of Buddhas seated on lion thrones beneath jeweled trees. They also saw Shakyamuni Buddha, together with the Thus Come One Many Jewels, seated on the lion throne within the jeweled *stupa*.

They further saw limitless, boundless, hundreds of thousands of myriads of *kotis* of Bodhisattvas Mahasattvas, as well as the four assemblies, reverently

circumambulating Shakyamuni Buddha. Having seen this, they greatly rejoiced, having gained what they had never had.

G5. Earthquakes.
G6. Seeing the entire great assembly.

Commentary:

The earth quaked in six ways—banging, roaring, cracking, shaking, rising, and surging—throughout the ten directions. The first three ways refer to sound; the second three refer to movement. This also represents the eyes, ears, nose, tongue, body, and mind, the six sense organs functioning in mutual interpenetration.

Each of the six types of earthquakes divides into three varieties: banging, universal banging, and equal universal banging. This applies to the other five kinds of quaking as well, thus making eighteen kinds in all, representing the eighteen realms.

And the living beings in those worlds—the gods, dragons, *yakshas, gandharvas, asuras, garudas, kinnaras*. *Kinnaras* are music spirits in the court of the Jade Emperor. They can also dance. Their music is millions of times better than music in the human realm. If people ever heard this music, they would fly. Their thoughts would fly off into heaven. ***Mahoragas*** are big pythons. They turned into snakes because although they cultivated, they didn't keep the precepts. There were **humans, nonhumans, and so forth,** who, **by means of the Buddha's** inconceivable **spiritual powers, all saw, in the Saha world, the limitless, boundless, hundreds of thousands of myriads of *kotis* of Buddhas seated on lion thrones beneath jeweled trees.** The lion thrones were five *yojanas* high. **They also saw Shakyamuni Buddha, together with the Thus Come One Many Jewels, seated on the lion throne within the jeweled *stupa*.**

They further saw limitless, boundless, hundreds of thousands of myriads of *kotis* of Bodhisattvas Mahasattvas, as well as the four assemblies, reverently circumambulating Shakyamuni Buddha. Having seen this, through the Buddha's great spiritual powers, **they greatly rejoiced, having gained what they had never had.** They had never witnessed such an inconceivable state before.

Sutra:

> **Just then the gods in space called out in a loud voice: "Passing from here through limitless, boundless, hundreds of thousands of myriads of *kotis* of *asamkhyeyas* of worlds, there is a country called Saha. Within it is a Buddha named Shakyamuni who now, for the sake of all the Bodhisattvas Mahasattvas, proclaims a Great Vehicle Sutra by the name of the *Wonderful Dharma Lotus Flower*, a Dharma for teaching Bodhisattvas, of whom the Buddha is protective and mindful. You should all rejoice deep within your hearts, bow, and make offerings to Shakyamuni Buddha."**

G7. Calling out in space.

Commentary:

Just then the gods. Having just seen Shakyamuni Buddha in the Saha world being circumambulated by all the Bodhisattvas and other beings in the Saha world, the gods manifested great spiritual powers and spoke in space. The gods, dragons, and eightfold division passed on the word and **in space called out in a loud voice.** The voice sounded like thunder; all could hear it. It came through clearer than radio or television. And it said, **"Passing from here through limitless, boundless, hundreds of thousands of myriads of *kotis* of *asamkhyeyas* of worlds,** now hear this! Now hear this! **There is a country called Saha."** *Saha* means "able to be endured," because the living beings in that world really know how to cultivate patience. It's so bitter, and still they can take it. So we are pretty good, hanging in here in the Saha world practicing the Bodhisattva path. It's so much suffering, but we can still stand it. **"Within it is a Buddha named Shakyamuni who now, for the sake of all the Bodhisattvas Mahasattvas** and the Arhats, too, **proclaims a Great Vehicle Sutra by the name of *Wonderful Dharma Lotus Flower*,** the great Dharma of the real mark, the wonderful Sutra of the Great Vehicle. The Dharma is wonderful and the vehicle is great. It is the Great Vehicle's *Wonderful Dharma Lotus Flower Sutra*. The Wonderful Dharma is as beautiful and immaculate as a lotus flower, which grows up out of the mud but is not defiled. This king of Sutras is **a Dharma for teaching Bodhisattvas**. So we are now hearing the Great Vehicle *Wonderful Dharma Lotus Flower Sutra,* a teaching for great Bodhisattvas. Even though we have not yet realized the fourth fruit of Arhatship, we have already heard the Bodhisattva Dharma, **of whom the Buddhas are protective and mindful.** The Buddhas are protective of this Sutra, and if you recite it, they are protective and mindful of you. If you recite the *Dharma Flower Sutra,* the Buddhas of the ten directions will be protective and mindful of you. If you obtain the wonderful doctrine of the *Dharma Flower Sutra,* you will develop wisdom and your stupidity will disappear. If it weren't that the Buddhas were being protective and mindful of you, how could you get so intelligent? It's because you recite the *Dharma Flower Sutra* that you gain this kind of wisdom, wisdom like the sea. Wouldn't you say this was wonderful? **You should all rejoice deep within your hearts.** All of you should bring forth the great Bodhi resolve, bring forth the mind of true Prajna and rejoice in the merit and virtue of this Sutra, **bow, and make offerings to Shakyamuni Buddha** in the Saha world."

Sutra:

> **Hearing this sound in space, all the living beings placed their palms together, faced the Saha world, and said, "Namo Shakyamuni Buddha! Namo Shakyamuni Buddha!"**

G8. Taking refuge from afar.

Commentary:

Hearing this sound in space, this amazing voice booming through the air, **all the living beings placed their palms together.** The Bodhisattvas and Arhats may have spiritual powers, but common folks don't. This sound, however, was heard not only by the Bodhisattvas and Arhats, but by the common people as well. All the living beings thought, "This is truly inconceivable. They are telling us from empty space that Shakyamuni Buddha has appeared in the Saha world. Let's put our palms together and face that world which is 'able to be endured.'" And from such a long distance away they **faced the Saha world and said, "Namo Shakyamuni Buddha! Namo Shakyamuni Buddha!"** Shakyamuni Buddha is our teacher. After this, if someone asks you who your teacher is, just say, "Shakyamuni Buddha," because that's correct. If they say you are being evasive, you can say, "You just don't understand the Buddhadharma."

Sutra:

> **And then from afar, they scattered all kinds of flowers, incense, beads, banners, canopies, ornaments for the body, and precious and rare objects on the Saha world. The objects they scattered came from the ten directions like clouds gathering, and turned into jeweled canopies, completely covering the Buddhas in that region.**

G9. Making offerings from afar.

Commentary:

And then from afar, they scattered all kinds of flowers, incense, beads, millions of **banners, canopies, ornaments for the body, and precious and rare objects on the Saha world.** "Ornaments for the body" refers to caps and clothing, which are used to adorn the body. If you run out into the street without wearing any clothes, even though this is a free country, the police will stop you and ask what you are doing. The gods sent down very nice-looking and beautiful clothing. They didn't follow the current American fashion of buying new clothes and cutting holes in them. That's really stupid. Why would you cut a hole in your sleeve and another one in your pants before wearing them? You think that shows you're an old cultivator, wearing such tattered clothes? That's extremely stupid. People who do this are just too confused. They don't know the difference between right and wrong. The young people start a fad, competing to cut holes in their clothes. You cut one hole, he cuts two, and others cut three, four, and five holes, even to the point of deliberately exposing the private parts of their bodies. The point of wearing clothes is to cover up those parts, but they cut holes there. Wouldn't you say that was stupid? This competition in stupidity—this new fad—is really a joke. You shouldn't wear clothing that's too fancy, but you shouldn't dress too poorly either. And you shouldn't destroy your clothes, cutting holes in them for no good reason. **The objects they scattered came from the ten directions like gathering clouds, and turned into jeweled canopies completely covering the Buddhas in that region.** They covered Shakyamuni Buddha, the division-body Buddhas, and Many Jewels Buddha.

Sutra:

> **Then the worlds of the ten directions interpenetrated without obstruction, as if they were one Buddhaland.**

G10. The ten directions interpenetrating as if they were one Buddhaland.

Commentary:

Then the worlds of the ten directions, the other limitless worlds, **interpenetrated without obstruction.** The worlds of the ten directions joined into one world; one world was just the worlds of the ten directions. In this world, we don't know the situation in other worlds. But at that time, when Shakyamuni Buddha was speaking the *Dharma Flower Sutra*, the worlds of the ten directions united into one world. One world and the worlds of the ten directions had no distinctions. They penetrated one another without impediment, **as if they were one Buddhaland.** Shakyamuni Buddha appeared in the Saha world, and the Saha world and the worlds of the ten directions became one world.

Sutra:

> **At that time the Buddha told Superior Conduct and all the great assembly of Bodhisattvas, "The spiritual power of all the Buddhas is limitless, boundless, and inconceivable like this. If, using these spiritual powers, I were to speak of the meritorious virtues of this Sutra for limitless, boundless, hundreds of thousands of myriads of *kotis* of *asamkhyeyas* of eons by way of entrustment, I could not finish."**

E3. Conclusion: Exhortation to uphold the Sutra.
F1. Praising and entrusting.

Commentary:

At that time the Buddha told Superior Conduct Bodhisattva and all the great assembly of Bodhisattvas, all the Bodhisattvas who had welled forth out of the earth and the Bodhisattvas who came with the division-body Buddhas, **"The spiritual power of all the Buddhas is limitless, boundless, and inconceivable like this. If, using these spiritual powers, I were to speak of the meritorious virtues of this Sutra for limitless, boundless, hundreds of thousands of myriads of *kotis* of *asamkhyeyas* of eons by way of entrustment,** so as to urge living beings to receive, uphold, read, recite, and propagate the *Dharma Flower Sutra,* **I could not finish."**

Sutra:

> **"In general, all the Dharmas of the Thus Come One, all the sovereign spiritual powers of the Thus Come One, all the secret storehouses of the Thus Come One, all the extremely profound deeds of the Thus Come One are all proclaimed and revealed in this Sutra."**

F2. Entrustment in general.

Commentary:

In general, all the Dharmas of the Thus Come One, all the sovereign spiritual powers of the Thus Come One, all the secret storehouses of the Thus Come One. The *Dharma Flower Sutra* is the secret storehouse and contains all of the Buddha's Dharmas. **All the extremely profound deeds of the Thus Come One are all proclaimed and revealed in this Sutra.** All the Dharma that I did not speak during the past over forty years of my teaching is contained in this final *Dharma Flower Sutra*. No one had ever understood this Dharma, and now it's plainly revealed. I am revealing it to you all. It's not like before when I held back the wonderful Dharma and did not speak it. Now I proclaim it.

Sutra:

> **"Therefore, all of you, after the passing of the Thus Come One, should with a single mind receive, uphold, read, recite, and explain it, write it out, and cultivate it as spoken. Those who receive, uphold, read, recite,**

explain, write out, and cultivate it as spoken, in whatever land they may be, in a place where the Sutra is kept: whether in a garden, in a forest, or beneath a tree; in a Sangha dwelling; in the dwelling of the white-robed; in a palace or hall; or in the mountains, valleys, or wilderness—in all of these places they should build a *stupa* and make offerings."

F3. Exhortation and entrustment.

Commentary:

Therefore, all of you, after the passing of the Thus Come One, should with a single mind receive, uphold, read, recite, and explain it, write it out, and cultivate it as spoken. In cultivation the most important thing is to be single-minded. No matter what you do, you should turn to one. Don't have two minds. If you have two minds, there's no response. Those who believe in the Buddha should do so with one mind and have no doubts. Don't think, "Is there really a Buddha? Wouldn't it be better to be a Catholic or some kind of Protestant?" If you're that scattered, no matter what you do, you won't gain merit and virtue or accomplishment. So you must turn your mind to one.

Now we're having a Guanyin Session. You could say that this is a Dharma hard to meet in a hundred thousand myriad eons. You shouldn't think that it's so simple to recite "Namo Guanshiyin Pusa." For every line you recite, there is one line of advantage gained. The "Universal Door Chapter" says, "If a person has much desire and always recites, reverently, the name of Guanyin Bodhisattva, he will be separated from desire." Isn't that a great advantage? If you have a lot of desire and lust, then your mind will not be peaceful. How do you leave desire? By reciting the name of Guanyin Bodhisattva.

"If a person has much hatred and always recites, reverently, the name of Guanyin Bodhisattva, he will be separated from hatred." Let's say there's a person who gets mad all the time and rages with the fire of ignorance, like a tiger—very fierce. It's said,

The fire of ignorance,
The spirit of a tiger,
Are the results of offenses
Committed in the past.

If you always recite Guanyin Bodhisattva's name, your hatred will decrease.

I'll tell you something. I used to have a bigger temper than anyone. I was always getting mad at people. If I wasn't beating them, then I was yelling at them. I've told you this many times. When I was little I loved to hit and scold people. No matter who they were, they had to submit to me. Anyone who refused to follow my orders got clobbered. Now I no longer like to hit or scold people. I don't know how I got rid of my anger, but it's gone.

"Sure, we know, we know," you say. "He's still got a big temper!"

You never saw it when it was really big! It would have scared you to death. I got rid of my temper by reciting the name of Guanyin Bodhisattva.

"If a person is very stupid, but always recites reverently the name of Guanyin Bodhisattva, he will be separated from stupidity." Now we are having a Guanyin Session and everyone—left-home people and laypeople—should recite if you have time. Don't fail to participate. If you are especially busy or tied up with some business, that's one thing. Otherwise, laypeople who aren't working should come and recite. If you recite one phrase, it's better than earning a hundred dollars a day. You shouldn't think, "What use is reciting Guanyin Bodhisattva's name?" It's very useful.

"But if I earn a hundred dollars, I can buy things to eat. If I recite Guanyin Bodhisattva's name, that's not going to fill me up when I'm hungry."

That's because you don't have a true heart. If you had a true heart, you would automatically become full. Not only would you be full, but when Guanyin Bodhisattva gave you some sweet dew, you would recite and feel it was sweeter than honey. If you don't recite, you won't attain this state; but if you do recite, it will happen naturally. I am definitely not cheating you. If you are sincere and recite Guanyin Bodhisattva's name, it's sweeter than eating candy. You don't know about the good points, and so you think you can goof off or make phone calls or do other things. You are just wasting precious time and not being single-minded. Concentrating on one thing, you forget everything else. You forget about eating; you forget about wearing clothes: all that remains is the one sentence, "Namo Guanshiyin Pusa." If you can be like that, then Guanshiyin Bodhisattva will pour sweet dew on your crown, pat you on the head, and say, "You are really a good kid. Good boy! Good girl! Bring forth the great resolve for Bodhi. I'll help you. Cultivate the true, and you'll get a share, make progress in the Way, and be free from demons."

Then your cultivation will be successful. But you have to be sincere. And so the present Sutra passage says, "with a single mind receive it, uphold it, read it, recite it, explain it, and write it out, and cultivate it as spoken." You cultivate in accord with the doctrines in the *Dharma Flower Sutra*.

"What doctrine is that?" you ask.

I've told you a million times! It's a doctrine wonderful beyond words. You forgot it? Never-Slighting Bodhisattva bowed whenever he met anyone, saying, "I dare not slight you, for you will all become Buddhas." Note that he said, "*You* will become Buddhas." He didn't say, "*I* am a Buddha." He forgot himself. He was cultivating according to the doctrines in the *Dharma Flower Sutra*.

"Those who receive, uphold, read, recite, explain, write out, and cultivate it as spoken, in whatever land they may be, in a place where the Sutra is kept: whether in a garden or a pavilion, **in a forest, or beneath a tree; in a Sangha dwelling; in the dwelling of the white-robed,** that is, at a layperson's home; **in a palace or hall,** such as a Buddha hall or a lecture hall; **or in the mountains, valleys, or** a desolate **wilderness—in all of these places they should build a** adorned ***stupa*** **and make offerings."**

Sutra:

> **"For what reason? You should know that this place is a Way-place wherein all Buddhas gain *anuttarasamyaksambodhi,* wherein all Buddhas turn the Dharma-wheel, and wherein all Buddhas enter Nirvana."**

F4. Explaining the entrustment.

Commentary:

For what reason? You should know that this place is a Way-place wherein all Buddhas gain *anuttarasamyak-sambodhi,* wherein all Buddhas turn the Dharma-wheel, and wherein all Buddhas enter Nirvana. "Wherein" here refers not to a place, but to the *Dharma Flower Sutra*. It was just in the *Dharma Flower Sutra* that the Buddhas gained Unsurpassed, Proper and Equal, Right Enlightenment. It was just because all the Buddhas received, upheld, read, recited, explained, and wrote out the *Dharma Flower Sutra* that they turned the Dharma-wheel. Lecturing the *Dharma Flower Sutra* is turning the Dharma-wheel. The Buddhas of the ten directions, within the *Dharma Flower Sutra,* turn the great Dharma-wheel and enter Nirvana, obtaining the four virtues of Nirvana: permanence, bliss, true self, and purity.

Sutra:

At that time the World Honored One, wishing to restate this meaning, spoke verses, saying,

The Buddhas, ones who save the world,
Dwelling in great spiritual penetrations,
In order to delight living beings,
Manifest limitless spiritual powers.
Their tongues reach to the Brahma Heavens,
Their bodies emit countless lights.
They make appear these rare events
For the sake of those who seek the
Buddha Way.
The sounds made when the Buddhas cough
And the sounds made when they snap their fingers

Are heard throughout the lands of
the ten directions
As the earth quakes in six ways.
Since after the Buddha's passing
One can uphold this Sutra,
All Buddhas rejoice
And display limitless spiritual powers.

D2. Verses.
E1. Verses about spiritual power.

Commentary:

At that time the World Honored One, being very compassionate and **wishing to restate this meaning** in a very simple form, **spoke verses, saying,** ***"The Buddhas, ones who save the world,*** who are greatly kind and compassionate and rescue all from suffering and difficulty, wish to save all living beings." ***Dwelling in great spiritual penetrations.*** The Buddhas have great spiritual powers, and so they are able to rescue living beings. If they were just like ordinary people, what would they use to rescue living beings with? So they use the power of great spiritual penetrations.

In order to delight living beings, they ***manifest limitless spiritual powers. / Their tongues reach to the Brahma Heavens***. They put forth their vast and long tongues, which reach all the way up to the Great Brahma Heaven. ***Their bodies emit countless lights***, light of countless colors. ***They make appear these rare events, / For the sake of those who seek the Buddha Way.***

The sounds made when the Buddhas cough / And the sounds made when they snap their fingers. These sounds are very soft, but all of the living beings throughout the ten directions can hear them. For example, if the *weinuo* [the person in charge of starting and ending a meditation sit] has entered samadhi or has fallen asleep and it's time to end the sit, you can snap your fingers and he will awaken. The Buddhas make these sounds to wake living beings up. They clear their throats or snap their fingers, signaling to living beings that they shouldn't remain asleep, living drunk and dying in a dream.

These kinds of sounds ***are heard throughout the lands of the ten directions / As the earth quakes in six ways.*** All the lands in the ten directions quake in six ways—banging, roaring, shaking, cracking, surging, rising—which are auspicious portents.

Since after the Buddha's passing / One can uphold this Sutra, the *Dharma Flower Sutra,* ***all Buddhas,*** World Honored Ones, ***rejoice / And display limitless spiritual powers.***

Sutra:

> ***In order to bequeath this Sutra,***
> ***He praises those who receive and hold it.***
> ***Doing so throughout limitless eons,***
> ***Still he cannot finish.***
> ***The merit and virtue of these people***
> ***Is boundless and infinite,***
> ***Like space in the ten directions,***
> ***Without any boundary.***

E2. Conclusion.
F1. Praise.

Commentary:

In order to bequeath this Sutra, Shakyamuni Buddha wanted to hand on the teaching to the Bodhisattvas and living beings, exhorting them to receive and uphold this Sutra. "Bequeath" means to pass on some work, to appoint someone to a job. Shakyamuni Buddha is appointing all the Bodhisattvas as keepers and propagators of the *Dharma Flower Sutra.*

He praises those who receive and hold it. / Doing so throughout limitless eons, / Still he cannot finish. / The merit and virtue of these people / Is boundless and infinite and eternal, ***like space in the ten directions.*** Where are the boundaries of space? They can't be found. The merit and virtue of reciting the *Dharma Flower Sutra* is also like space—it is ***without any boundary.***

Someone says, "Space is empty! There's nothing there. Is our merit and virtue also empty and nonexistent?"

Space is nonexistent. However, if you can understand this "nonexistence" then you can understand "all of existence." Besides, this analogy isn't comparing the merit and virtue to space by its nonexistence, but rather because it is boundless and infinite. Basically, within true emptiness, there is wonderful existence. Wonderful existence cannot be seen, but you can't presume that because you cannot see it, it doesn't exist. It truly exists—you just don't understand it.

Sutra:

> ***Those who can uphold this Sutra***
> ***Have already seen me***
> ***And also seen the Buddha Many Jewels***
> ***And all of the division bodies.***

They also see me on this day
Teaching and transforming the
Bodhisattvas.

F2. Explaining the meaning of the entrustment.
G1. All the Dharmas.

Commentary:

Those who can uphold this Sutra—who can receive, uphold, read, recite, write out, and explain the *Dharma Flower Sutra* —***have already seen me.*** They have seen my true body ***and also seen the Buddha Many Jewels / And all of the division bodies,*** the Buddhas who are division bodies of Shakyamuni Buddha. ***They also see me on this day,*** here with Many Jewels Thus Come One in the jeweled *stupa,* ***teaching and transforming the Bodhisattvas.***

Sutra:

Those who can uphold this Sutra
Cause me and my division bodies
And the previous Buddha, Many Jewels,
To all rejoice.
They shall also see and make offerings
To the Buddhas of the ten directions—
in the present,
The past, and the future—
Causing them to rejoice as well.

G2. Comfort and spiritual powers.

Commentary:

Those who can uphold this Sutra / Cause me and my

division bodies / And the previous Buddha, Many Jewels, / To all rejoice. / They shall also see and make offerings / To the Buddhas of the ten directions—in the present, / The past, and the future— / Causing them to rejoice as well. The Buddhas throughout the ten directions will be happy.

Sutra:

> ***The secret and essential Dharma obtained***
> ***By the Buddhas seated in their Way-places***
> ***Will also be gained before too long***
> ***By those who can uphold this Sutra.***

G3. The secret storehouse.

Commentary:

The secret and essential Dharma—their secret treasuries—***obtained / By the Buddhas seated in their Way-places / Will also be gained before too long / By those who can uphold this Sutra.*** Why? Because they read and recite the *Dharma Flower Sutra.*

Sutra:

> ***Those who can uphold this Sutra***
> ***Will take delight in speaking, without end,***
> ***The meaning of the Dharmas,***
> ***Their names and expressions,***
> ***Like the wind blowing through space,***
> ***Without obstacle.***
> ***After the Thus Come One's passing,***
> ***They will understand the Sutras spoken***
> ***by the Buddha,***

The causes and conditions in sequence,
And speak them truly, according with
their meanings.
Like the light of the sun and moon
Dispelling all darkness,
These people walk through the world
Dispersing the darkness of living beings,
Teaching limitless Bodhisattvas
Ultimately to dwell in the One Vehicle.

G4. The profound work.

Commentary:

Those who can uphold this Sutra, who can read, recite, explain, and write out the *Dharma Flower Sutra,* ***will take delight in speaking, without end, / The meaning of the Dharmas, / Their names and expressions, / Like the wind blowing through space, / Without obstacle.*** He will gain the Four Kinds of Unobstructed Eloquence: Unobstructed Eloquence of Expression, Unobstructed Eloquence of Meaning, Unobstructed Eloquence of Dharma, and Unobstructed Eloquence of Delight in Speech. He shall speak with unobstructed eloquence like the wind in space, blowing where it will, without obstacles.

After the Thus Come One's passing, / They will understand the Sutras spoken by the Buddha. They will deeply enter the Sutra store and gain wisdom like the sea. They will understand ***the causes and conditions in sequence, and speak them truly, according with their meanings***—according with the doctrine of the real mark.

Like the light of the sun and moon / Dispelling all darkness, / These people walk through the world / Dispersing the

darkness of living beings, helping living beings get rid of their stupidity. Basically living beings don't understand, they are confused. They take day to be night, sleeping during the day and running around at night. I have seen a lot of people like this. They are like cats prowling around at night. They are also like mice that hide in their holes during the day and run around at night looking for food. But a person who upholds the *Dharma Flower Sutra* is intent on ***teaching limitless Bodhisattvas / Ultimately to dwell in the One Vehicle*** and attain Buddhahood.

Sutra:

> ***Therefore, those with wisdom,***
> ***Hearing the advantages of this***
> ***merit and virtue,***
> ***Should, after my passing,***
> ***Receive and uphold this Sutra.***
> ***These people most certainly and***
> ***without a doubt***
> ***Will attain the Buddha Way.***

F3. Exhortation.

Commentary:

Therefore, those with wisdom, / Hearing the advantages of this merit and virtue, / Should, after my passing,—after I enter Nirvana, ***receive and uphold this Sutra. / These people most certainly and without a doubt / Will obtain the Buddha Way.*** They will certainly attain Buddhahood. There's no doubt about it.

End of Chapter Twenty-one

The Thus Come One is greatly kind and compassionate, without stinginess and without fear. He is able to give living beings the wisdom of the Buddha, the wisdom of the Thus Come One, and spontaneous wisom. The Thus Come One is a great giving host to all living beings.

The Wonderful Dharma Lotus Flower Sutra

Chapter Twenty-two: The Entrustment

Sutra:

AT THAT TIME Shakyamuni Buddha rose from his Dharma seat and manifested great spiritual power. With his right hand he patted the crowns of limitless Bodhisattvas Mahasattvas and said, "Throughout limitless hundreds of thousands of myriads of *kotis* of *asamkhyeyas* of eons, I have cultivated and practiced the rare Dharmas of *anuttarasamyaksambodhi*. I now entrust them to all of you. You should, with a single mind, propagate this Dharma, causing it to spread and grow extensively."

In this way he patted the Bodhisattvas Mahasattvas on the crown three times, saying, "Throughout limitless hundreds of thousands of myriads of *kotis* of *asamkhyeyas* of eons, I have cultivated and practiced the rare Dharmas of *anuttarasamyaksambodhi*. I now entrust them to all of you. You should receive, uphold, read, recite, and

vastly proclaim this Dharma, causing all living beings to hear and understand it.

"For what reason? The Thus Come One is greatly kind and compassionate, without stinginess and without fear. He is able to give living beings the wisdom of the Buddha, the wisdom of the Thus Come One, and spontaneous wisdom. The Thus Come One is a great giving host to all living beings. You should all accordingly study the Dharmas of the Thus Come One and never be stingy.

"In the future, if there is a good man or a good woman who believes in the Thus Come One's wisdom, you should expound the Dharma Flower Sutra to that person, causing the person to hear and understand and obtain the Buddha's wisdom. If there are living beings who do not believe or accept it, you should instruct them with another of the profound Dharmas of the Thus Come One, benefiting them and causing them to rejoice. If you can do this, you will have already repaid the kindness of the Buddhas."

When the Bodhisattvas Mahasattvas heard the Buddha's words, profuse joy permeated their bodies. With increasing reverence, they bowed their heads, placed their palms together, faced the Buddha, and said in unison, "We shall reverently carry out the World Honored One's command. Yes, World Honored One, pray do not be concerned about this." The assembly of Bodhisattvas Mahasattvas spoke in this way three times, saying, "We shall reverently carry out the Buddha's command. Yes, World Honored One, pray do not be concerned about this."

At that time Shakyamuni Buddha sent the division-body Buddhas of the ten directions back to their own lands, saying, "Peace to all of you Buddhas. Let the *stupa* of the Buddha Many Jewels be again as it was."

As he said this, the limitless division-body Buddhas of the ten directions, seated on lion thrones beneath jeweled trees; the Buddha Many Jewels; Superior Conduct and the limitless *asamkhyeyas* of Bodhisattvas in the great assembly; Shariputra and the other Hearers; as well as the fourfold assembly and all those in the world—the gods, humans, asuras, and so forth—hearing the Buddha's words, all rejoiced exceedingly.

Chapter Twenty-two: The Entrustment

A Simple Explanation by the Venerable Master Hsuan Hua

Sutra:

AT THAT TIME Shakyamuni Buddha rose from his Dharma seat and manifested great spiritual power. With his right hand he patted the crowns of limitless Bodhisattvas Mahasattvas and said, "Throughout limitless hundreds of thousands of myriads of *kotis* of *asamkhyeyas* of eons, I have cultivated and practiced the rare Dharmas of *anuttarasamyaksambodhi*. I now entrust them to all of you. You should, with a single mind, propagate this Dharma, causing it to spread and grow extensively."

In this way he patted the Bodhisattvas Mahasattvas on the crown three times, saying, "Throughout limitless hundreds of thousands of myriads of *kotis* of *asamkhyeyas* of eons, I have cultivated and practiced the rare Dharmas of *anuttarasamyaksambodhi*. I now entrust them to all of you. You should receive, uphold, read, recite, and vastly proclaim this Dharma, causing all living beings to hear and understand it."

C2. The Thus Come One pats the Bodhisattvas on the head and entrusts the Sutra to them.
D1. The entrustment.
E1. The Thus Come One's entrustment.
F1. The entrustment proper.

Commentary:

This is Chapter Twenty-two of the *Dharma Flower Sutra*, entitled "The Entrustment." What is the purpose of this chapter? The Sutras spoken by the Buddha are Dharmas used to teach and transform living beings. These Dharmas must be propagated and circulated.

What does "entrustment" mean? Shakyamuni Buddha gives commands to all the Bodhisattvas and Arhats, telling them that the propagation and circulation of the *Dharma Flower Sutra* should be their responsibility in the future.

Why should the *Dharma Flower Sutra* be circulated? Because this is a most important Sutra. When living beings without good roots hear even one sentence, one word, or one verse of the *Dharma Flower Sutra*, they can plant good roots. Those living beings who have already planted good roots, who hear even one word, one sentence, or one verse of the *Dharma Flower Sutra* can increase their good roots. Those living beings whose good roots have already increased, hearing one word, one sentence, or one verse, will bring their good roots to maturity. Those living beings whose good roots have already matured, hearing one word, one sentence, or one verse of the *Dharma Flower Sutra*, will obtain liberation. But, they must hear the *Dharma Flower Sutra*—one word, one sentence, one verse, one chapter, or the entire Sutra. If they don't hear it, they can't obtain liberation. The *Dharma Flower Sutra* is the Wonderful

Dharma. Because of this, any kind of living being who obtains the doctrine of the *Dharma Flower Sutra* can obtain the due advantages.

Shakyamuni Buddha entrusted the Bodhisattvas, Arhats, Bhikshus, and Bhikshunis with some hard work. He enlisted them to propagate and circulate the *Dharma Flower Sutra,* to distribute it to places it had not gone before, like water flowing into the great sea. Printing the Sutras is also a method of distribution. When Sutras are printed, you don't just print up one for your own use. There is great merit and virtue in printing the Sutras; it causes your original wisdom to open up. When you print a Sutra for yourself, you open up your own wisdom. If you print up ten, twenty, a hundred or more copies, you can give them to your relatives and friends as gifts, all wrapped up nicely for New Year's or Christmas or whatever. You can write a card saying, "This is something I really find hard to part with, but I am giving it to you. It's hard to part with because it is extremely fine and wonderful. I read it and it chased all my stupidity away. It brought my wisdom back! So this is my best Dharma experience." When they get the card, they will think, "He really didn't want to part with this," and they won't throw it away.

If you say something like this, "Here, take this thing. I've read it enough. I don't want it. It's of no use to me, so you take it," then they won't want it either. They won't even look at it; they will just throw it away. That's not a good approach for distribution. You can use various methods to get them to accept the Sutra. When they get it and read it, they too will open up their wisdom, return from confusion, and go towards enlightenment. You will have saved that person. Since you saved that person, in the future when you become a Buddha that person will be your Dharma protector; he will be your disciple, because you benefited him. Propagating the Sutras requires all kinds of methods. Shakyamuni Buddha spoke the Sutras and then entrusted the work of propagation to his disciples. He said, "In the future you should lecture the *Dharma Flower Sutra,* receive and uphold it, read and recite it. All of you Bodhisattvas should write it out and explain it to others. Disseminate it. When I enter Nirvana, exhaust your efforts to spread the teachings among the people."

There's a simple analogy: Take our magazine, *Vajra Bodhi Sea*. I tell you, "Hurry up and get it out. Do the mailing early." That's just a form of entrustment. Probably you all understand from this example. It's just an encouragement to get going. Perhaps you and I were in the assembly with Shakyamuni Buddha and heard this entrustment, and so now we are here lecturing on the Sutra, listening to it, reading it, reciting it, and writing it out. We have received the entrustment from Shakyamuni Buddha, and that's what we are taking care of—listening and lecturing. So we are just following Shakyamuni Buddha's instructions.

Entrustment is just propagation. The Dharma-protecting laypeople at the Sino-American Buddhist Association and the Buddhist Lecture Hall are going to print the *Sixth Patriarch's Dharma Jewel Platform Sutra,* which is easy to read because it has a commentary. I feel that Americans have a great affinity with this Sutra, so everyone should bring forth a Great Vehicle Bodhi resolve, not a Small Vehicle resolve, to print this Sutra. A Great Vehicle resolve means to practice giving Dharma. The gift of Dharma surpasses all other gifts, including gifts of money, but it needs the gift of money to make it possible. You first use money to print the Sutra, and then you can give the Sutra to people. You may not know how to lecture on Sutras, but if you give people this Sutra with its commentary, you accrue the same merit and virtue as if you lectured on it.

Since this lecture hall is very small, not many people can come to the lectures. If too many people come and there aren't enough seats, they have to stand through the lecture, which is very uncomfortable. If you give this Dharma gift to your friends and relatives, then even if they can't come to the lectures, they can read the Sutra and learn a little bit of Buddhadharma. In this way you can lead them to bring forth the resolve for Bodhi. And so I hope all of you will contribute however much you can to print the *Sixth Patriarch's Sutra*. Each person should print at least ten copies. If you can print a hundred, a thousand, or ten thousand copies, then that's even better.

I always supported the printing of Sutras when I was in Hong Kong. When I first arrived in Hong Kong, there were very few Sutras. First I printed the *Lotus Sutra* and the *Shurangama Sutra*. The copies of the *Shurangama Sutra* that we used here were printed in Hong Kong then. Later on other Buddhist organizations followed my example, and now Hong Kong has lots of Sutras.

At present there are very few Sutras in America, but now we are starting to print Sutras. Everyone should print a lot of Sutras. Printing Sutras is a way of propagating the Buddhadharma. It opens up your wisdom. Why hasn't your wisdom opened yet? Because you have little merit and virtue. If you had a lot of merit and virtue, you would be wise and enlightened. The reason you are so confused is that you lack merit and virtue.

"I've liberated creatures, printed Sutras, and made offerings to the Triple Jewel. Why am I confused if I've done all these meritorious deeds?" you ask. You think you've done a lot of merit, but actually it's very little. Think for a moment: Do you spend more money on meritorious deeds or more on food, clothing, and a place to live? You've spent so much money on these three mundane affairs, yet you don't feel it's a lot. Then you make a small contribution to print Sutras or liberate living creatures and you think you're creating great merit and virtue. How much money do you squander on gambling and drugs? Do you spend more to buy a car or more to create merit? Do you spend more money taking vacations or more on merit and virtue? Take stock of yourself and see how much merit you have.

These figures aren't that easy to calculate, so go home tonight and calculate them, and then bring forth a great Bodhi resolve tomorrow. If someone volunteers to print a thousand or ten thousand copies of the Sutra, one for every person in America, then he is one who takes the entrustment to propagate the Buddhadharma seriously. I believe that tomorrow, or on Guanyin Bodhisattva's anniversary, someone will definitely offer to print, if not a hundred thousand copies, then ten thousand copies; if not ten thousand, then one thousand, or one hundred at the minimum. I myself will print a hundred copies for the Way-place. We can sell them for fifteen dollars each and use the money to pay the temple's bills. Although I don't know how to do business, this is a pretty good deal. But it's to help Buddhism, not myself. I myself don't need anyone's help, and I don't need to do anything either. That's all I want to say about printing Sutras. You should mine this treasure. Don't just laugh and forget what I've said.

This evening when we do the Great Transference of Merit, you should walk faster during the walking recitation. It's called "running to the Western Land." You have to walk faster and recite faster. Recite as if you're in a hurry, and hit the fish faster. Our place is small, but in a bigger place people would walk twice as fast as the normal walking speed. Whoever is not busy should come to attend the Guanyin Session. Guanyin Sessions, Chan Sessions, and Buddha Recitation Sessions are equally important. You shouldn't think there's no point in reciting Guanyin Bodhisattva's name. As we recite and sit, there is stillness within movement and movement within stillness. You can cultivate in stillness, or you can cultivate in movement. Movement and stillness do not hinder each other. It's a perfect Dharma door. Don't misunderstand the Buddhadharma and think some of it is good and some is not. The Dharma is all the same; there is no good or bad. Whether you think it's good or bad is just your own opinion, but the Budhadharma itself is all equal.

At that time, when the Buddha had finished the chapter "The Spiritual Powers of the Thus Come One" and was about to speak this chapter, "The Entrustment," **Shakyamuni Buddha rose from his Dharma seat and manifested great spiritual power. With his right hand he patted the crowns of limitless Bodhisattvas Mahasattvas and said, "Throughout limitless hundreds of thousands of myriads of *kotis* of *asamkhyeyas* of eons, I have cultivated and practiced the rare Dharmas of *anuttarasamyaksambodhi*.**

They are extremely hard to meet in a million eons. These Dharmas of the Unsurpassed, Proper and Equal, Right Enlightenment are just the Dharmas of the *Dharma Flower Sutra*. **I now entrust them to all of you. You should, with a single mind, propagate this Dharma, causing it to spread and grow extensively,** and causing people to understand it."

In this way he patted the Bodhisattvas Mahasattvas on the crown of their heads **three times, saying, "Throughout limitless hundreds of thousands of myriads of *kotis* of *asamkhyeyas* of eons, I have cultivated and practiced the rare Dharmas of *anuttarasamyaksambodhi*. I now entrust them to all of you.** I give you this job. **You should receive, uphold, read, recite, and vastly proclaim this Dharma, causing all living beings to hear and understand it."**

Sutra:

> **"For what reason? The Thus Come One is greatly kind and compassionate, without stinginess and without fear. He is able to give living beings the wisdom of the Buddha, the wisdom of the Thus Come One, and spontaneous wisdom. The Thus Come One is a great giving host to all living beings. You should all accordingly study the Dharmas of the Thus Come One and never be stingy."**

F2. The explanation.

Commentary:

For what reason? It's because **the Thus Come One is greatly kind and compassionate.** With his kindness he bestows happiness. With his compassion he relieves us of suffering. He is **without stinginess**, not miserly when it comes to giving the gift of Dharma. **And** he is **without fear. He is able to give living beings the wisdom of the Buddha**; the Buddha's wisdom is that of great enlightenment. **The wisdom of the Thus Come One** is the Buddha's Great Perfect Mirror Wisdom; **and spontaneous wisdom** is the original wisdom of the self-nature. **The Thus Come One is a great giving host to all living beings.** He gives all his Dharma treasures to living beings. **You should all accordingly study the Dharmas of the Thus Come One.** You great Bodhisattvas should imitate the Buddha **and never be stingy.** Once you have learned the Dharma, don't be niggardly with it.

Sutra:

> **"In the future, if there is a good man or a good woman who believes in the Thus Come One's wisdom, you should expound the *Dharma Flower Sutra* to that person, causing the person to hear and understand and obtain the Buddha's wisdom. If there are living beings who do not believe or accept it, you should instruct them with another of the profound Dharmas of the Thus Come One, benefiting them and causing them to rejoice. If you can do this, you will have already repaid the kindness of the Buddhas."**

F3. Exhortation and entrustment.

Commentary:

In the future, if there is a good man or a good woman, one who cultivates the five precepts and the ten good deeds, **who believes in the Thus Come One's wisdom, you should**

expound the ***Dharma Flower Sutra*** **to that person, causing him or her to hear and understand** it, **and** to **obtain the Buddha's wisdom.**

If there are living beings who do not believe or accept it, you should instruct them with another of the profound Dharmas of the Thus Come One, benefiting them and causing them to rejoice. Lecture some other deep and wonderful Sutra. Teach and transform them so that they gain benefit and are happy. **If you can do this,** then **you will have already repaid the kindness of the Buddhas** of the ten directions.

Sutra:

> **When the Bodhisattvas Mahasattvas heard the Buddha's words, profuse joy permeated their bodies. With increasing reverence, they bowed their heads, placed their palms together, faced the Buddha, and said in unison, "We shall reverently carry out the World Honored One's command. Yes, World Honored One, pray do not be concerned about this." The assembly of Bodhisattvas Mahasattvas spoke in this way three times, saying, "We shall reverently carry out the Buddha's command. Yes, World Honored One, pray do not be concerned about this."**

E2. The Bodhisattvas accept the command.

Commentary:

When the Bodhisattvas Mahasattvas heard the Buddha's words, profuse joy permeated their entire **bodies. With increasing reverence**—they were twice as respectful—**they bowed their heads, placed their palms together, faced the**

Buddha, and said in unison, "We shall reverently carry out the World Honored One's command. Yes, World Honored One, pray do not be concerned about this. We will comply, just as you wish. Please don't worry about this, Buddha." **The assembly of Bodhisattvas Mahasattvas spoke in this way three times, saying, "We shall reverently carry out the Buddha's command. Yes, World Honored One, pray do not be concerned about this."**

Sutra:

> **At that time Shakyamuni Buddha sent the division-body Buddhas of the ten directions back to their own lands, saying, "Peace to all of you Buddhas. Let the *stupa* of the Buddha Many Jewels be again as it was."**

E3. The job finished, and the call to disband.

Commentary:

At that time Shakyamuni Buddha sent the division-body Buddhas of the ten directions back to their own lands, saying, "Peace to all of you Buddhas. You can all go back to your own lands. We have taken care of business. You can all go back home now. **Let the *stupa* of the Buddha Many Jewels be again as it was."** The *stupa* of the Buddha Many Jewels has certified the speaking of the *Dharma Flower Sutra*, and now it is time for it to return to the lower direction, where it originally came from.

Sutra:

> **As he said this, the limitless division-body Buddhas of the ten directions, seated on lion thrones beneath jeweled trees; the Buddha Many Jewels; Superior**

Conduct and the limitless *asamkhyeyas* of Bodhisattvas in the great assembly; Shariputra and the other Hearers; as well as the fourfold assembly and all those in the world—the gods, humans, *asuras,* and so forth—hearing the Buddha's words, all rejoiced exceedingly.

D2. Rejoicing.

Commentary:

As he said this, the limitless division-body Buddhas of the ten directions, seated on lion thrones beneath jeweled trees; the Buddha Many Jewels; Superior Conduct Bodhisattva; **and the limitless *asamkhyeyas* of Bodhisattvas in the great assembly; Shariputra and the other Hearers; as well as the fourfold assembly and all those in the world—the gods, humans, *asuras,* and so forth,** including the eightfold division—**hearing the Buddha's words, all rejoiced exceedingly.**

End of Chapter Twenty-two

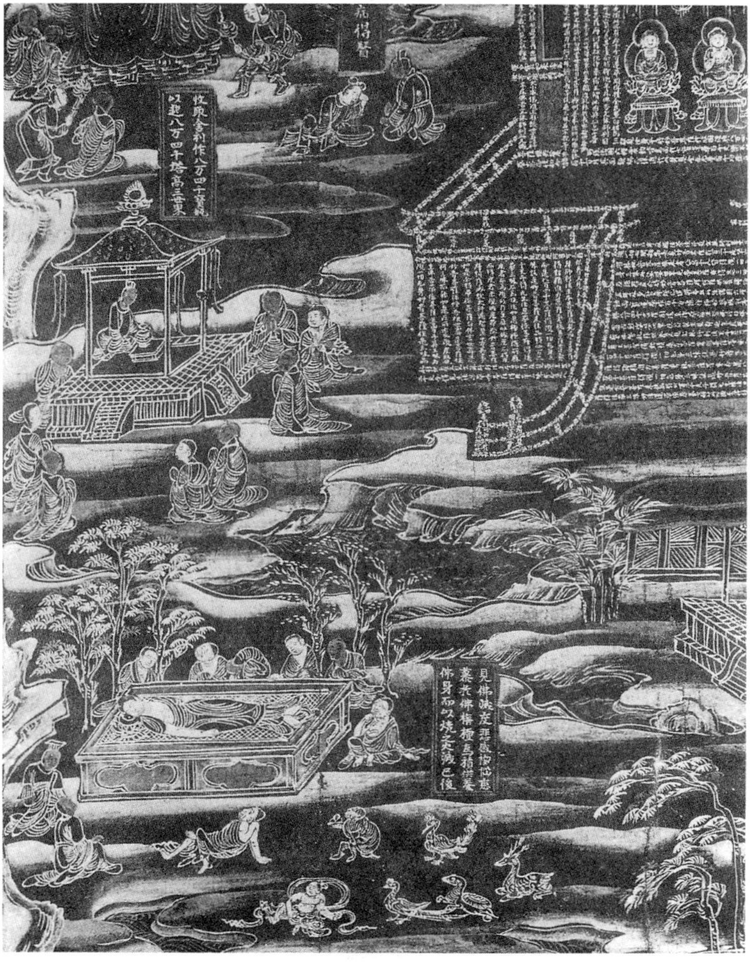

Seeing the Buddha pass into stillness, the Bodhisattva was sorely grieved and longed for the Buddha. He then built a pyre of "this shore" *chandana* incense as an offering to that Buddha's body and set it on fire. When the fire had consumed itself, he collected the sharira; made eighty-four thousand jeweled urns; and built eighty-four thousand *stupas.*

The Wonderful Dharma Lotus Flower Sutra

Chapter Twenty-three: The Former Deeds of Medicine King Bodhisattva

Sutra:

AT THAT TIME THE Bodhisattva Constellation King Flower spoke to the Buddha, saying, "World Honored One, how is it that the Bodhisattva Medicine King roams throughout the Saha world? World Honored One, Medicine King Bodhisattva has undertaken so many hundreds of thousands of myriads of *kotis* of *nayutas* of bitter practices, so difficult to practice.

"It would be excellent, World Honored One, if you would please explain a bit. On hearing this, all the gods, dragons, *yakshas, gandharvas, asuras, garudas, kinnaras, mahoragas,* humans, nonhumans, and so forth, and the Bodhisattvas who have come from other lands, as well as the assembly of Hearers, will rejoice."

The Buddha then told the Bodhisattva Constellation King Flower, "Once, as many eons ago as there are grains of sand in limitless Ganges Rivers, there was a Buddha by the name of Virtue Pure and Bright Like the Sun and Moon, Thus Come One, One Worthy of Offerings, One of Right and Universal Knowledge, One Perfect in Clarity and Conduct, Well Gone One Who Understands the World, Unsurpassed Lord, Regulating Hero, Teacher of Humans and Gods, Buddha, World Honored One. That Buddha had eighty *kotis* of great Bodhisattvas Mahasattvas and a great assembly of Hearers, equal in number to the sand grains in seventy-two Ganges Rivers. His life span as a Buddha was forty-two thousand eons. The life spans of the Bodhisattvas were the same. In his country there were no women, hell-beings, hungry ghosts, animals, or *asuras*, and so forth, and also no difficulties. The ground was as level as the palm of one's hand, made of *vaidurya*, adorned with jeweled trees, covered with jeweled nets, and hung with beautiful banners. It was surrounded everywhere with precious vases and censers. There were terraces made of the seven gems, one terrace for each tree, the trees being separated from the terraces by a distance of an arrow's flight. Beneath each tree sat Bodhisattvas and Hearers. Upon each of the terraces were hundreds of *kotis* of gods playing heavenly music and singing praises to the Buddha as an offering."

At that time that Buddha, for the sake of the Bodhisattva All Beings Delight in Seeing, as well as for the host of Bodhisattvas and the host of Hearers, spoke the *Dharma Flower Sutra*.

The Bodhisattva All Beings Delight in Seeing enjoyed practicing ascetic practices. Within the Dharma of the Buddha Virtue Pure and Bright Like the Sun and Moon, he applied himself with vigor, single-mindedly seeking Buddhahood for a full twelve thousand years. He then obtained the samadhi of the manifestation of all physical forms.

Having obtained this samadhi, his heart rejoiced greatly and he immediately thought, "I have obtained the samadhi of the manifestation of all physical forms. This is through the power of having heard the *Dharma Flower Sutra*. I should now make an offering to the Buddha Virtue Pure and Bright Like the Sun and Moon, and to the *Dharma Flower Sutra*."

He then entered that samadhi, and as an offering to the Buddha, he rained down *mandarava* flowers and *mahamandarava* flowers from space. Finely ground, hard, black *chandana* also filled the sky and descended like clouds. And there rained the incense of 'this shore' *chandana*, six *karshas* of which are worth the entire Saha world, as an offering to the Buddha.

Having made this offering he arose from samadhi. He thought to himself, "Although by means of spiritual powers I have made this offering to the Buddha, it is not as good as offering my body." He then swallowed incense of many kinds—*chandana, kunduruka, turushka, prikka,* aloeswood, and resin incense. He also drank the oil of *champaka* and other flowers for a full twelve hundred years. He smeared himself with fragrant oil, and in the presence of the Buddha Virtue Pure and Bright Like the Sun and Moon, he wrapped himself in heavenly jeweled robes and poured fragrant oil over himself. Then by means of spiritual penetration power and vows, he burned his own body. The light shone everywhere throughout worlds in number to the grains of sand in eighty *kotis* of Ganges Rivers.

Within them all, the Buddhas simultaneously praised him, saying, "Good indeed! Good indeed! Good man, this is true vigor. This is called a true Dharma offering to the Thus Come One. Offerings of flowers, incense, beads, burning incense, ground incense, paste incense, heavenly cloth, banners, canopies, 'this shore' *chandana* incense, and all such offerings of various kinds cannot come up to it. If one gave away one's countries, cities, wives, and children, that also could not match it. Good man, this is called foremost giving. Among all gifts, it is the most honored and most supreme, because it is an offering of Dharma to the Thus Come Ones." Having uttered these words, they became silent.

His body burned for twelve hundred years, after which time it was consumed.

When the Bodhisattva All Beings Delight in Seeing had made this Dharma offering and his life had come to an end, he was born again. In the country of the Buddha Virtue Pure and Bright Like the Sun and Moon, in the household of the King Pure Virtue, he was born suddenly by transformation, seated in full lotus.

He immediately spoke this verse to his father:

Your Majesty, you should now know:
I, cultivating in that place,
All at once attained
The samadhi of the manifestation of
all forms.

Diligently practicing great vigor,
I renounced the body I cherished
As an offering to the World
Honored One,
In order to seek supreme wisdom.

Having spoken this verse, he said to his father, "The Buddha Virtue Pure and Bright Like the Sun and Moon is still present from of old. Formerly, after making an offering to that Buddha, I gained the *dharani* of understanding the speech of all living beings. I further heard the *Dharma Flower Sutra* with its eight hundred thousand myriads of *kotis* of *nayutas* of *kankaras, vivaras, akshobhyas,* and so forth of verses. Great King, I should now return and make offerings to this Buddha."

Just then he sat on a platform made of the seven treasures, rose up into space to the height of seven *tala* trees, went into the Buddha's presence, bowed with his head at the Buddha's feet, placed his ten fingers together, and spoke this verse in praise of the Buddha:

How amazing and rare the countenance,
With its light shining in ten directions!
I formerly made offerings
To you whom I now behold once again.

When the Bodhisattva All Beings Delight in Seeing had spoken this verse, he then spoke to the Buddha, saying, "World Honored One! World Honored One! You are still in the world!"

The Buddha Virtue Pure and Bright Like the Sun and Moon told the Bodhisattva All Beings Delight in Seeing,

"Good man, the time of my Parinirvana has arrived. The time for my passing into stillness has arrived. You can arrange my couch, for tonight I shall enter Parinirvana."

He further commanded the Bodhisattva All Beings Delight in Seeing, saying, "Good man, I entrust you, all the Bodhisattvas and great disciples, with the Buddhadharma and also with the Dharma of *anuttarasamyaksambodhi*. I also entrust to you the worlds of the seven treasures throughout the three thousand great thousand world systems, with their jeweled trees, jeweled terraces, and gods-in-waiting. After my passing into stillness, I also entrust you with all my *sharira*. You should distribute them and vastly make offerings to them. You should build several thousand *stupas*."

In this way, the Buddha Virtue Pure and Bright Like the Sun and Moon, having commanded the Bodhisattva All Beings Delight in Seeing, in the last watch of the night entered Nirvana.

Seeing the Buddha pass into stillness, the Bodhisattva was sorely grieved and longed for the Buddha. He then built a pyre of 'this shore' *chandana* incense as an offering to that Buddha's body and set it on fire. When the fire had consumed itself, he collected the *sharira*; made eighty-four thousand jeweled urns; and built eighty-four thousand *stupas*, three worlds in height, adorned with poles from which hung banners, canopies, and many jeweled bells.

The Bodhisattva All Beings Delight in Seeing then further thought to himself, "Although I have made this offering, my heart is not yet satisfied. I should now make further offerings to the *sharira*." He then spoke to the

dragons, the *yakshas,* and so forth in the great assembly, saying, "All of you pay attention and bring your thoughts to one, for I am now going to make offerings to the *sharira* of the Buddha Virtue Pure and Bright Like the Sun and Moon." Having said that, in front of the eighty-four thousand *stupas,* as an offering he burned his arms, with their adornments of a hundred blessings, for seventy-two thousand years, thereby causing countless multitudes of hosts seeking to be Hearers and limitless *asamkhyeyas* of people to bring forth the resolve for *anuttarasamyak-sambodhi,* and enabling them to dwell in the samadhi of the manifestation of all physical forms.

At that time all the Bodhisattvas, gods, humans, *asuras,* and so forth, seeing him without arms, were smitten with grief and said, "The Bodhisattva All Beings Delight in Seeing is our teacher. He has taught and transformed us, but now his arms are burned off and his body deformed."

Then the Bodhisattva All Beings Delight in Seeing made this vow amidst the great assembly, saying, "Having renounced both of my arms, I should certainly attain the Buddha's golden-colored body. If this is true and not false, both of my arms should now be restored to as they were before."

After he had made this vow, his arms were spontaneously restored. This came about through the purity and depth of this Bodhisattva's blessings, virtue, and wisdom.

The three thousand great thousand world system then quaked in six ways. The heavens rained down jeweled flowers, and all the humans and gods gained what they had never had before.

The Buddha told the Bodhisattva Constellation King Flower, "What do you think? Was the Bodhisattva All Beings Delight in Seeing anyone else? He was just the present Medicine King Bodhisattva. Gifts of his body, such as this one, number in the limitless hundreds of thousands of myriads of *kotis* of *nayutas*.

"Constellation King Flower! If a person who brings forth the resolve desiring to obtain *anuttarasamyaksambodhi* can burn off a finger or a toe as an offering to a Buddha *stupa*, his offering will surpass that of one who uses as offerings countries, cities, wives, and children or even the three thousand great thousand worlds with their mountains, forests, rivers, ponds, and precious objects.

"If, further, a person filled the three thousand great thousand world system with the seven treasures and offered it to the Buddha, to the great Bodhisattvas, Pratyekabuddhas, and Arhats, the merit and virtue that person would obtain would not be equal to that of one who receives and upholds even a single four-line verse of the *Dharma Flower Sutra*, for the latter's blessings are greater by far.

"Constellation King Flower! Just as, for example, among all the streams, rivers, and bodies of water, the ocean is foremost, so, too, among all the Sutras spoken by the Thus Come One, the *Dharma Flower Sutra* is the deepest and greatest.

"Further, just as among Earth Mountain, Black Mountain, the Lesser Iron Ring Mountain, the Greater Iron Ring Mountain, the Ten Jeweled Mountains, and the entire multitude of mountains, Mount Sumeru is foremost, so, too, among all the Sutras, the *Dharma Flower Sutra* is the most supreme.

"Further, just as among the stars, the Moon God is foremost, so, too, among the thousands of myriads of *kotis* of kinds of Sutra Dharmas, the *Dharma Flower Sutra* shines the brightest.

"Further, just as the Sun God can disperse all darkness, so, too, this Sutra can disperse all the darkness of unwholesomeness.

"Further, just as among the minor kings, the Wheel-Turning Sage King is foremost, so, too, among the Sutras, this Sutra is the most honored.

"Further, just as in the Heaven of the Thirty-three, Lord Shakra is king, so, too, among the Sutras, this Sutra is king.

"Further, just as the great Brahma God is the father of all living beings, so, too, is this Sutra the father of all the worthy sages, those studying, those beyond study, as well as those who have brought forth the Bodhisattva mind.

"Further, just as among the common people, the Srota-apanna, Sakridagamin, Anagamin, Arhat, and Pratyekabuddha are foremost, so, too, among all Sutra Dharmas, whether spoken by the Thus Come Ones, by the Bodhisattvas, or by Hearers, this Sutra is foremost.

"One who can receive and uphold this Sutra, in the same way, is foremost among all living beings.

"Just as among all the Hearers and Pratyekabuddhas, the Bodhisattva is foremost, so, too, among all the Sutra Dharmas, this Sutra is foremost.

"Just as the Buddha is the king of all Dharmas, so, too, is this Sutra the king of all Sutras.

"Constellation King Flower! This Sutra can save all living beings. This Sutra can lead all living beings to separate from suffering and distress. This Sutra can greatly benefit all living beings, fulfilling their vows. Just as a clear, refreshing pool can quench the thirst of all; as a cold person finds fire; as a naked person finds clothing; as a merchant finds customers; as a child finds its mother; as a passenger finds a boat; as a sick person finds a doctor; as one in a dark place finds a lamp; as a poor person finds a jewel; as the people find a king; as a trader finds the sea; as a torch dispels darkness—the *Dharma Flower Sutra*, in the same way, can cause living beings to leave all suffering and all sickness and pain; it can untie all the bonds of birth and death.

"If a person hears the *Dharma Flower Sutra*, writes it out himself, or employs others to write it out, the limits of the merit and virtue he shall obtain cannot be calculated even by means of the Buddha's wisdom.

"If a person writes out this Sutra and makes offerings to it of flowers; incense; beads; burning incense; powdered incense; paste incense; banners and canopies; clothing; and lamps of various kinds such as butter lamps, oil lamps and fragrant oil lamps, lamps of *champaka* oil, lamps of *sumana* oil, lamps of *patala* oil, lamps of *varshika* oil, and lamps of *navamalika* oil, the merit and virtue obtained is also limitless.

"Constellation King Flower, if a person hears this chapter, "The Past Deeds of Medicine King Bodhisattva," he will also obtain limitless, boundless merit and virtue. If a woman hears this chapter, "The Past Deeds of Medicine King Bodhisattva," and is able to receive and uphold it, after quitting this woman's body, she will not undergo one again. If, after the passing of the Thus Come One, in the last five hundred years, there is a woman who, hearing this Sutra, can cultivate according to its teachings, at the end of her present life, she will go straight to the blissful world of the Buddha Amitayus, where she is surrounded by great Bodhisattvas. Born from a lotus flower, seated on a jeweled seat, this person will never again be tormented by desire, tormented by hate and stupidity, or tormented by the filth of arrogance and jealousy. He will obtain the Bodhisattva's spiritual penetrations and the patience with the nonproduction of dharmas. Having obtained this patience, his eye will be pure. By means of this pure eye, he will see Buddhas, Thus Come Ones, equal in number to the grains of sand in seven million two thousands *kotis* of *nayutas* of Ganges Rivers.

"At that time all the Buddhas will praise this person from afar saying, 'Good indeed, good indeed, good man, that within the Dharma of Shakyamuni Buddha you can receive, uphold, read, recite, and ponder this Sutra, and speak it for others. The merit and virtue you obtain is limitless and boundless. Fire cannot burn it. Water cannot flood it. Your merit and virtue is such that if a thousand Buddhas spoke of it together, they could not exhaust it.

"'You have already been able to destroy the thieves of Mara, to ruin the troops of birth and death, and to demolish all remaining enemies.

"'Good man, a hundred thousand Buddhas, with their power of spiritual penetrations, all protect you. In all the world with its gods and humans, there is none like you, with the exception of the Thus Come One. The Hearers and Pratyekabuddhas, and even the Bodhisattvas, cannot equal you in wisdom and Dhyana concentration.'

"Constellation King Flower, such is the power of the merit and virtue and wisdom accomplished by this Bodhisattva.

"If a person hears this chapter, "The Past Deeds of Medicine King Bodhisattva," and rejoices in accord, praising its goodness, that person's mouth in his present life will always emit the fragrance of a blue lotus. The pores of his body will always emit the perfume of oxhead *chandana*. The merit and virtue he obtains will be as described above.

"Therefore, Constellation King Flower, I entrust to you this chapter, "The Past Deeds of Medicine King Bodhisattva." After my passing, in the last five hundred years, propagate it extensively in Jambudvipa. Do not let it become extinct, thereby allowing evil demons, demonic denizens, all the heavenly dragons, *yakshas, kumbhandas,* and so forth to get their way.

"Constellation King Flower, you should use the power of spiritual penetrations to protect this Sutra. Why? Because this Sutra is good medicine for the sicknesses of those in Jambudvipa. If a sick person gets to hear this Sutra, his sickness will be cured immediately. He will not grow old or die.

"Constellation King Flower, if you see a person who receives and upholds this Sutra, you should scatter blue lotuses filled with powdered incense over him as an offering. Having done that, you should reflect: 'Before long, this person will certainly lay out a grass mat, sit in the Way-place, vanquish the troops of Mara, blow the

Dharma conch, strike the great Dharma drum, and save all living beings from the sea of old age, sickness, and death. Therefore, when those who seek the Buddha Way see one who receives and upholds this Sutra, they should bring forth a reverent heart in this way."

When this chapter, "The Past Deeds of Medicine King Bodhisattva," was spoken, eighty-four thousand Bodhisattvas obtained the *dharani* of understanding the speech of all living beings.

From within the jeweled *stupa,* the Thus Come One Many Jewels praised Constellation King Flower Bodhisattva, saying, "Good indeed, good indeed, Constellation King Flower! You have accomplished such inconceivable merit and virtue that you are able to question Shakyamuni Buddha about matters such as these and to benefit limitless living beings.

Chapter Twenty-three: The Former Deeds of Medicine King Bodhisattva

A Simple Explanation by the Venerable Master Hsuan Hua

Sutra:

AT THAT TIME the Bodhisattva Constellation King Flower spoke to the Buddha, saying, "World Honored One, how is it that the Bodhisattva Medicine King roams throughout the Saha world? World Honored One, Medicine King Bodhisattva has undertaken so many hundreds of thousands of myriads of *kotis* of *nayutas* of bitter practices, so difficult to practice.

"It would be excellent, World Honored One, if you would please explain a bit. On hearing this, all the gods, dragons, *yakshas, gandharvas, asuras, garudas, kinnaras, mahoragas,* humans, nonhumans, and so forth, and the Bodhisattvas who have come from other lands, as well as the assembly of Hearers, will rejoice."

B2. Teaching others and exhorting to propagation.

C1. Chapter on "Medicine King"—Master of Propagating Dharma.
D1. The question.

Commentary:

This chapter talks about the very bitter and difficult ascetic practices of Medicine King Bodhisattva. These are ascetic practices most people could not perform. He has already been certified to the fruit and become a Bodhisattva. Before, he wasn't called Medicine King Bodhisattva; he was called the Bodhisattva All Beings Delight in Seeing. When beings saw him they felt happy in their eyes, happy in their ears, happy in their noses, happy in their mouths, happy in their bodies, and, of course, even happier in their minds. Why? It was because this Bodhisattva developed affinities with all living beings, and so they all liked to see him. No matter whether they believed in the Buddha or not, they liked to see him. And so he was called the Bodhisattva All Beings Delight in Seeing. When they saw him, their hearts felt happy. Even children loved to see him. Perhaps he always gave them candy. In any case, he never gave the kids hot peppers, so they liked him. Not only did people like him, but all the animals liked him, too.

This Bodhisattva used his body as an offering to the Buddha. How did he do this? He didn't cut off all his flesh and offer it to the Buddha for a meal, or lie in front of the Buddha on the altar as an offering. He drank a lot of fragrant oil, wrapped his body in oil-soaked cotton, set it on fire, and sat there like a human candle as an offering to the Buddha.

"Did it hurt?" you ask.

I believe it hurt, yes, but he could bear it. He could offer up his body to the Buddha. I also believe it didn't hurt. Why not? Because he had already forgotten all about his own body. The light of the wisdom of his self-nature had come forth. He knew that the body is just a false combination of the four elements—earth, air, fire, and water—and so it didn't hurt. In general, hurting or not hurting, he could give up his body as an offering to the Buddha. This is a genuine offering to the Buddha with nothing false in it at all. And so the text says, "This is true vigor." To say nothing of burning up our whole bodies, we couldn't even burn off an arm. Sometimes people burn off one, two, three, four, five, or six fingers for the Buddha. But no one has ever burned off an arm.

"Okay, I'll try it out," you say.

Don't try it out. First cultivate patience. When you have true samadhi power, you can do something like this. If you don't have true samadhi power, it's going to hurt, and it will be useless because you won't be able to practice true renunciation. Medicine King Bodhisattva practiced such difficult ascetic deeds.

Medicine King Bodhisattva made a vow to cure all living beings of their illnesses. No matter what sickness you have, he wants to help you, because he is very compassionate. His **former deeds** refer to the actions he cultivated in the past, the ascetic practices he undertook.

At that time the Bodhisattva Constellation King Flower spoke to the Buddha, saying, "World Honored One, I heard about Medicine King Bodhisattva in the *Shurangama Sutra* Assembly, but there are a few things I haven't completely understood. **How is it that the Bodhisattva Medicine King roams throughout the Saha world?** How is it that he has such affinities with the living beings in the Saha world? **World Honored One, Medicine King Bodhisattva has undertaken so many hundreds of thousands of myriads of *kotis* of *nayutas* of bitter practices, so difficult to practice.** He cures living beings' illnesses. In past lives he must surely have cultivated many ascetic practices, making vows to save living beings from the pain of sickness. These bitter practices were beyond the capabilities of ordinary people.

It would be excellent, World Honored One, if you would please explain this **a bit.** You don't have to tell the whole thing; that would take too long. Just give us a general idea. **On hearing this, all the gods, dragons, *yakshas, gandharvas, asuras, garudas, kinnaras, mahoragas,* humans, nonhumans, and so forth, and the Bodhisattvas who have come from other lands, as well as the assembly of Hearers, will rejoice.** They all want to hear about the bitter practices of Medicine King Bodhisattva."

Sutra:

> **The Buddha then told the Bodhisattva Constellation King Flower, "Once, as many eons ago as there are grains of sand in limitless Ganges Rivers, there was a Buddha by the name of Virtue Pure and Bright Like the Sun and Moon, Thus Come One, One Worthy of Offerings, One of Right and Universal Knowledge, One Perfect in Clarity and Conduct, Well Gone One Who Understands the World, Unsurpassed Lord, Regulating Hero, Teacher of Humans and Gods, Buddha, World Honored One. That Buddha had eighty *kotis* of great Bodhisattvas Mahasattvas and a great assembly**

of Hearers, equal in number to the sand grains in seventy-two Ganges Rivers. His life span as a Buddha was forty-two thousand eons. The life spans of the Bodhisattvas were the same. In his country there were no women, hell-beings, hungry ghosts, animals, or *asuras*, and so forth, and also no difficulties. The ground was as level as the palm of one's hand, made of *vaidurya*, adorned with jeweled trees, covered with jeweled nets, and hung with beautiful banners. It was surrounded everywhere with precious vases and censers. There were terraces made of the seven gems, one terrace for each tree, the trees being separated from the terraces by a distance of an arrow's flight. Beneath each tree sat Bodhisattvas and Hearers. Upon each of the terraces were hundreds of *kotis* of gods playing heavenly music and singing praises to the Buddha as an offering."

D2. The answer.
E1. Answering only about the ascetic practices.
F1. The origins.

Commentary:

Hearing the Bodhisattva Constellation King Flower's question, **the Buddha then told the Bodhisattva Constellation King Flower, "Once, as many eons ago as there are grains of sand in limitless Ganges Rivers, there was a Buddha by the name of Virtue Pure and Bright Like the Sun and Moon, Thus Come One, One Worthy of Offerings, One of Right and Universal Knowledge, One Perfect in Clarity and Conduct, Well-Gone One Who Understands the**

World, Unsurpassed Lord, Regulating Hero, Teacher of Humans and Gods, Buddha, World Honored One. That Buddha had eighty *kotis* of great Bodhisattvas Mahasattvas whom he had taught and transformed. **And a great assembly of Hearers, equal in number to the sand grains in seventy-two Ganges Rivers. His life span as a Buddha was forty-two thousand eons. The life spans of the Bodhisattvas were the same. In his country there were no women,** because all the living beings were born purely from lotus flowers, with pure bodies. Nor were there any **hell-beings, hungry ghosts, animals, or *asuras,*** who love to fight, **and so forth,** referring to the others of the eightfold division. **And also** there were **no difficulties**—none of the eight difficulties. **The ground was as level as the palm of one's hand.** Why was the ground level? Because the people's hearts were level. When people's hearts aren't level, there are mountains, valleys, ravines, and seas, and rivers. It's people's minds that create these things. If people's minds are level, then the earth is perfectly flat. It was **made of *vaidurya,*** and **adorned with jeweled trees, covered with jeweled nets, and hung with beautiful banners. It was surrounded everywhere with precious vases and censers. There were** magnificent **terraces made of the seven gems, one terrace for each tree, the trees being separated from the terraces by a distance of an arrow's flight. Beneath each tree sat Bodhisattvas and Hearers. Upon each of the terraces were hundreds of *kotis* of gods playing heavenly music and singing praises to the Buddha as an offering,** just as we sing the "Incense Praise" and other songs to the Buddha.

Sutra:

> **At that time that Buddha, for the sake of the Bodhisattva All Beings Delight in Seeing, as well as for the host of Bodhisattvas and the host of Hearers, spoke the *Dharma Flower Sutra*.**

F2. Past affairs.
G1. The Buddha speaks the Dharma.

Commentary:

At that time that Buddha, Virtue Pure and Bright Like the Sun and Moon, **for the sake of the Bodhisattva All Beings Delight in Seeing, as well as for the host of Bodhisattvas and the host of** great **Hearers, spoke the *Dharma Flower Sutra*.**

Sutra:

> **The Bodhisattva All Beings Delight in Seeing enjoyed practicing ascetic practices. Within the Dharma of the Buddha Virtue Pure and Bright Like the Sun and Moon, he applied himself with vigor, single-mindedly seeking Buddhahood for a full twelve thousand years. He then obtained the samadhi of the manifestation of all physical forms.**

G2. Cultivating offerings.
H1. Offerings in the present life.
I1. Cultivating and obtaining the Dharma.

Commentary:

The Bodhisattva All Beings Delight in Seeing enjoyed practicing ascetic practices. Within the Dharma of the

Buddha Virtue Pure and Bright Like the Sun and Moon, he applied himself with vigor. He was very vigorous and cultivated hard, **single-mindedly seeking Buddhahood for a full twelve thousand years.** So you have cultivated for two and a half years. How does that compare? From this passage we can see that one doesn't succeed in one's cultivation of the Bodhisattva path in a mere one or two years. **He then obtained the samadhi of the manifestation of all physical forms.** This means he could turn himself into all kinds of living beings in order to teach those kinds of beings. To save a person, he could turn himself into a person. Seeing a dog, he could turn himself into a dog. He could manifest in the body of any kind of living being. That was the kind of concentration power he obtained.

To save evil people, he would turn into an evil person. To save a good person, he would turn into a good person. He could turn into any kind of living being in order to teach it. If you want to do evil, he will turn into an evildoer to save you. After the evil deeds are done, he will say, "This isn't so great. Let's change from the evil and go towards the good." He will save you in that way. If he were entirely different, he wouldn't be able to save that being. So if Chinese people want to save Americans, they should get reborn as Americans! A lot of you have done just that, but you don't know about it.

Sutra:

> **Having obtained this samadhi, his heart rejoiced greatly and he immediately thought, "I have obtained the samadhi of the manifestation of all physical forms. This is through the power of having heard the *Dharma***

***Flower Sutra.* I should now make an offering to the Buddha Virtue Pure and Bright Like the Sun and Moon, and to the *Dharma Flower Sutra.*"**

He then entered that samadhi, and as an offering to the Buddha, he rained down *mandarava* flowers and *mahamandarava* flowers from space. Finely ground, hard, black *chandana* also filled the sky and descended like clouds. And there rained the incense of 'this shore' *chandana,* six *karshas* of which are worth the entire Saha world, as an offering to the Buddha.

I2. Thinking to repay the Buddha's kindness.
J1. The power of samadhi and the offering.

Commentary:

Having obtained this samadhi, his heart rejoiced greatly, and he immediately thought, "I have obtained the samadhi of the manifestation of all physical forms. I can appear in any form at all! **This is through the power of having heard the *Dharma Flower Sutra.*** It's all because the Buddha spoke the *Dharma Flower Sutra* that I have such spiritual powers. **I should now make an offering to the Buddha Virtue Pure and Bright Like the Sun and Moon, and to the *Dharma Flower Sutra.*"**

He then entered that samadhi, and as an offering to the Buddha, he rained down *mandarava* flowers and *mahamandarava* flowers—little white flowers and big white flowers—**from space. Finely ground, hard, black *chandana* also filled the sky and descended like clouds. And there rained** down **the incense of 'this shore' *chandana,*** that is, *chandana* from Jambudvipa, **six *karshas* of which are worth the entire Saha world.** "*Karsha*" is a Sanskrit term of measurement. Six small pieces, in other words, are worth the entire Saha world. All of this was by way of making **an offering to the Buddha** Virtue Pure and Bright Like the Sun and Moon.

Sutra:

> **Having made this offering he arose from samadhi. He thought to himself, "Although by means of spiritual powers I have made this offering to the Buddha, it is not as good as offering my body." He then swallowed incense of many kinds—*chandana, kunduruka, turushka, prikka,* aloeswood, and resin incense. He also drank the oil of *champaka* and other flowers for a full twelve hundred years. He smeared himself with fragrant oil, and in the presence of the Buddha Virtue Pure and Bright Like the Sun and Moon, he wrapped himself in heavenly jeweled robes and poured fragrant oil over himself. Then by means of spiritual penetration power and vows, he burned his own body. The light shone everywhere throughout worlds in number to the grains of sand in eighty *kotis* of Ganges Rivers.**

J2. Burning his body as an offering.
K1. Burning his body.

Commentary:

Having made this offering he, the Bodhisattva All Beings Delight in Seeing, **arose from samadhi.** Basically one does not enter or leave samadhi. So why does the text say "arose"? It's because this samadhi was a state the Bodhisattva had attained. In this state there was no entering or leaving, but because he made an offering, **he thought to himself, "Although, by means of spiritual powers I have made this offering to the Buddha,** using the inconceivably wonderful power of spiritual penetrations, **it is not as good as offering my body,** my physical body. That would be even more true-hearted of me." **He then swallowed incense of many kinds—*chandana; kunduruka; turushka*** [olibanum], which means "white couch grass incense"; ***prikka,*** "clove incense"; very fragrant **aloeswood; and resin incense,** which resembles glue and is also called "pine incense". **He also drank the oil of** *champaka,* of yellow flowers, **and other flowers for a full twelve hundred years. He** then **smeared himself with fragrant oil, and in the presence of the Buddha Virtue Pure and Bright Like the Sun and Moon, he wrapped himself in heavenly jeweled robes,** made of the finest and most delicate material. He **poured fragrant oil over himself. Then by means of spiritual penetration power and vows, he** used the true fire of his samadhi to light himself on fire and **burned his own body. The light shone everywhere throughout worlds in number to the grains of sand in eighty *kotis* of Ganges Rivers.** All the Buddhas witnessed his offering.

Sutra:

> **Within them all, the Buddhas simultaneously praised him, saying, "Good indeed! Good indeed! Good man, this is true vigor. This is called a true Dharma offering to the Thus Come One. Offerings of flowers, incense, beads, burning incense, ground incense, paste incense, heavenly cloth, banners, canopies, 'this shore' *chandana***

incense, and all such offerings of various kinds cannot come up to it. If one gave away one's countries, cities, wives, and children, that also could not match it. Good man, this is called foremost giving. Among all gifts, it is the most honored and most supreme, because it is an offering of Dharma to the Thus Come Ones." Having uttered these words, they became silent.

K2. The Buddhas' praise.

Commentary:

Within them all, the Buddhas simultaneously praised him. All the Buddhas in worlds equal in number to the grains of sand in eighty *kotis* of Ganges Rivers praised him, **saying, "Good indeed! Good indeed!** Really good. **Good man, this is true vigor.** You are truly vigorous—vigorous in body and in mind. **This is called a true Dharma offering to the Thus Come One."**

When Great Master Zhi Zhe, third Patriarch of the Tiantai School, reached this sentence of text in his recitation, he entered samadhi. He obtained the *dharani* of a single revolution, which enabled him to understand all of the Sutras in a very short space of time. At that time he saw that the Magic Mountain Dharma assembly was still in progress. Shakyamuni Buddha was still present on Vulture Peak speaking the *Dharma Flower Sutra*.

The Buddhas said that to offer one's body to the Buddhas is a true Dharma offering. Someone might say, "How can you say that to offer one's body is true vigor and a true Dharma offering? Even though he ate a lot of incense and fragrant oils, and smeared himself with scented oil, still this physical, flesh body, no matter how much it's submerged in fragrant oil, when set on fire, is going to stink. How could all the Buddhas like a stench like that and even praise him for it?"

The Buddhas did not like the stench. They were pleased with his true mind. In order to make an offering like that, you've got to have a perfectly true heart and be able to truly put it all down. One must have seen through the body as being empty and obtained nonobstruction. Having seen it as empty, one must then see through that very emptiness as empty. This is the attainment of great liberation. Having obtained great liberation is an ultimate kind of offering. This is a true Dharma offering, true vigor. You shouldn't make the mistake of thinking the Buddha likes burned bodies as offerings. That's not it at all. The Buddhas praise him because he could see through and put down his body, that thing that can't be put down. This is a true Dharma offering to the Thus Come One.

Offerings of flowers, incense, beads, burning incense, ground incense, paste incense, heavenly cloth, banners, canopies, 'this shore' *chandana* incense, and all other **such offerings of various kinds cannot come up to it.** Such offerings in no way compare with the merit and virtue gained from offering one's body. **If one gave away one's countries, cities,** outer wealth, **wives and children, that also could not match it.** In no way could it match the offering of your own body. This is truly great merit. **Good man, this is called foremost giving**—the very best kind. **Among all gifts, it is the most honored and most supreme, because it is an offering of Dharma to the Thus Come**

Ones. It is a causal condition for the accomplishment of your Dharma body.

Having uttered these words, they became silent. Nobody said a word.

Sutra:

His body burned for twelve hundred years, after which time it was consumed.

K3. The length of time his body burned.

Commentary:

When the Bodhisattva All Beings Delight in Seeing, after eating incense and fragrant oils, consumed himself with the true fire of samadhi, which came about from the wonderful functioning of spiritual power, **his body burned for twelve hundred years, after which time it was consumed.**

Sutra:

When the Bodhisattva All Beings Delight in Seeing had made this Dharma offering and his life had come to an end, he was born again. In the country of the Buddha Virtue Pure and Bright Like the Sun and Moon, in the household of the King Pure Virtue, he was born suddenly by transformation, seated in full lotus.

H2. Offerings in his next life.
I1. Born in the king's household.

Commentary:

When the Bodhisattva All Beings Delight in Seeing had made this Dharma offering and his life had come to an

end, naturally he died. Then **he was born again in the country of the Buddha Virtue Pure and Bright Like the Sun and Moon, in the household of the King Pure Virtue. He was born suddenly by transformation, seated in full lotus.** Suddenly he was there, a little child.

Sutra:

He immediately spoke this verse to his father:

Your Majesty, you should now know:
I, cultivating in that place,
All at once attained
The samadhi of the manifestation of
all forms.
Diligently practicing great vigor,
I renounced the body I cherished
As an offering to the World Honored One,
In order to seek supreme wisdom.

Having spoken this verse, he said to his father, "The Buddha Virtue Pure and Bright Like the Sun and Moon is still present from of old. Formerly, after making an offering to that Buddha, I gained the *dharani* of understanding the speech of all living beings. I further heard the *Dharma Flower Sutra* with its eight hundred thousand myriads of *kotis* of *nayutas* of *kankaras, vivaras, akshobhyas,* and so forth of verses. Great King, I should now return and make offerings to this Buddha."

12. Telling of his past deeds.

Commentary:

He immediately spoke this verse to his father. If he was born by transformation, why did he have a father? He was born into the King's house, and so he took him as his father. Actually, those born by transformation have neither father nor mother.

Your Majesty, you should now know: / I, cultivating in that place, in the presence of the Buddha Virtue Pure and Bright Like the Sun and Moon, ***all at once attained*** by cultivating the doctrines of the *Dharma Flower Sutra, **the samadhi of the manifestation of all forms***. In this samadhi I could manifest in any kind of body. ***Diligently practicing great vigor, / I renounced the body I cherished***—I burned it. I did this ***as an offering to the World Honored One, / In order to seek supreme wisdom.*** I was seeking the Buddha's wisdom.

Having spoken this verse, he said to his father, "The Buddha Virtue Pure and Bright Like the Sun and Moon is still present from of old. Formerly, after making an offering to that Buddha, I gained the *dharani* of understanding the speech of all living beings. I could understand all the languages of living beings without even studying them. **I further heard the *Dharma Flower Sutra* with its eight hundred thousand myriads of *kotis* of *nayutas* of *kankaras, vivaras, akshobhyas,* and so forth of verses.** The Sanskrit words here refer to large units of measurement, of which there are fifty-two in Sanskrit. *Kankara* is the sixteenth large number. *Vivara* is the eighteenth number. *Akshobhya* is the twentieth number. "And so forth" refers to the rest of the units of measurement. **Great King, I should now return**

and make offerings to this Buddha. It's time for me to go back and make offerings to the Buddha Virtue Pure and Bright Like the Sun and Moon."

Sutra:

Just then he sat on a platform made of the seven treasures, rose up into space to the height of seven *tala* trees, went into the Buddha's presence, bowed with his head at the Buddha's feet, placed his ten fingers together, and spoke this verse in praise of the Buddha:

How amazing and rare the countenance,
With its light shining in ten directions!
I formerly made offerings
To you whom I now behold once again.

When the Bodhisattva All Beings Delight in Seeing had spoken this verse, he then spoke to the Buddha, saying, "World Honored One! World Honored One! You are still in the world!"

I3. Going to the Buddha's place.

Commentary:

When he had finished speaking with his father, **just then he sat on a platform made of the seven treasures** and **rose up into space to the height of seven *tala* trees.** One *tala* tree is about seven feet tall, so that was about forty-nine or fifty feet in the air. He **went into the Buddha's presence, bowed with his head at the Buddha's feet, placed his ten fingers together, and spoke this verse in praise of the Buddha:**

How amazing and rare the countenance, / With its light shining in the ten directions! / I formerly made offerings / To you whom I now behold once again.

"O Buddha! With your thirty-two marks and eighty subsidiary characteristics, your appearance is extremely fine. Before, when I was the Bodhisattva All Beings Delight in Seeing, I made offerings to you." After he burned his body as an offering, he was reborn and met the Buddha again.

When the Bodhisattva All Beings Delight in Seeing had spoken this verse, he then spoke to the Buddha, saying, "World Honored One! World Honored One! You are still in the world!" The Bodhisattva was extremely happy that he could see the Buddha in a second lifetime. He felt as happy as someone who sees his parents again after being apart from them for a long time. That's why he called out the Buddha's title twice.

Sutra:

The Buddha Virtue Pure and Bright Like the Sun and Moon told the Bodhisattva All Beings Delight in Seeing, "Good man, the time of my Parinirvana has arrived. The time for my passing into stillness has arrived. You can arrange my couch, for tonight I shall enter Parinirvana."

He further commanded the Bodhisattva All Beings Delight in Seeing, saying, "Good man, I entrust you, all the Bodhisattvas and great disciples, with the Buddhadharma and also with the Dharma of *anuttara-samyaksambodhi*. I also entrust to you the worlds of the seven treasures throughout the three thousand great thousand world systems, with their jeweled trees,

jeweled terraces, and gods-in-waiting. After my passing into stillness, I also entrust you with all my *sharira*. You should distribute them and vastly make offerings to them. You should build several thousand *stupas*."

In this way, the Buddha Virtue Pure and Bright Like the Sun and Moon, having commanded the Bodhisattva All Beings Delight in Seeing, in the last watch of the night entered Nirvana.

14. The Thus Come One's entrustment.

Commentary:

The Buddha Virtue Pure and Bright Like the Sun and Moon told the Bodhisattva All Beings Delight in Seeing, "Good man, the time of my Parinirvana has arrived. You showed up just in time today. **The time for my passing into stillness has arrived.** I have taught all those beings I was supposed to teach and transform, and it is now time for me to leave. **You can arrange my couch.** Get my bed all ready, **for tonight I shall enter Parinirvana."**

The Buddha was born in the daytime, which represents the sun shining throughout the world. The Buddha entered Nirvana at midnight, which is yin. And so we have yin and yang. When the Buddha entered Nirvana, the world was plunged into darkness. We don't mean that the world was dark immediately after the Buddha entered Nirvana, but that after the Buddhadharma becomes extinct, the world will be in darkness. After the Buddha enters Nirvana, the Buddhadharma is still in the world, and so the world is still bright. If there were no Buddhadharma, the world would be as dark as night. **He further commanded the Bodhisattva**

All Beings Delight in Seeing, saying, "Good man, I entrust you, all the Bodhisattvas and great disciples, with the Buddhadharma and also with the Dharma of *anuttara-samyaksambodhi*. Here's a little work for you."

I also entrust to you the worlds of the seven treasures throughout the three thousand great thousand world systems, with their jeweled trees, jeweled terraces, and gods-in-waiting. The jeweled trees represent the kings of vows; the jeweled terraces represent the emptiness of all dharmas. The gods-in-waiting served the Buddha, did house-cleaning for him, poured tea for him, and things like that.

After my passing into stillness, I also entrust you with all my *sharira*. You should distribute them and vastly make offerings to them. You should build several thousand *stupas*, as many as eighty-four thousand of them."

In this way the Buddha Virtue Pure and Bright Like the Sun and Moon, having commanded the Bodhisattva All Beings Delight in Seeing, in the last watch of the night, after midnight, **entered Nirvana.**

Sutra:

> **Seeing the Buddha pass into stillness, the Bodhisattva was sorely grieved and longed for the Buddha. He then built a pyre of 'this shore' *chandana* incense as an offering to that Buddha's body and set it on fire. When the fire had consumed itself, he collected the *sharira*; made eighty-four thousand jeweled urns; and built eighty-four thousand *stupas*, three worlds in height, adorned with poles from which hung banners, canopies, and many jeweled bells.**

15. Following orders.

J1. Building *stupas*.

Commentary:

Seeing the Buddha pass into stillness, the Bodhisattva All Beings Delight in Seeing **was sorely grieved,** cried, **and longed for the Buddha.** He couldn't stand to see the Buddha enter Nirvana. He was like Ananda—all he did was cry, "Why didn't I ask the Buddha to remain in the world? If I had asked him to, he might not have entered Nirvana!" He was struck with grief and thought himself incompetent. He longed for the Buddha and couldn't let him go.

He then built a pyre of 'this shore' *chandana* incense as an offering to that Buddha's body and set it on fire. This is that very expensive incense, six little pieces of which are worth the entire Saha world. In Suzhou, at Lingyan Mountain, when the Venerable Yinguang completed the stillness, he was cremated with regular sandalwood incense. There were crowds of people there, covering the entire mountain for a couple of miles. After the cremation, they found many *sharira* in the ashes. When they had gathered up all the *sharira*, one of his disciples showed up, looking for one, but they were all gone. He looked and looked and couldn't find one. He stayed there for two days, crying. After two days, a *sharira* showed up, the biggest one yet! He took it home to make offerings to it. So the Buddhadharma is an inconceivable thing. Whoever is truly sincere and true will obtain a response. Whoever is not sincere or true will not obtain a response. That disciple was especially reverent and faithful to the old Master, always wishing to see him. But after the Master went to Nirvana, he could no longer see him, so he cried and cried until he found a *sharira*.

When the fire had consumed itself and had died down, **he collected the** ***sharira,*** **made eighty-four thousand jeweled urns**, putting many *sharira* in each urn, **and built eighty-four thousand** ***stupas,*** the same number as were built for Shakyamuni Buddha by King Ashoka. They were **three worlds in height, adorned with poles from which hung banners, canopies, and many jeweled bells** made of gold and silver.

Sutra:

> **The Bodhisattva All Beings Delight in Seeing then further thought to himself, "Although I have made this offering, my heart is not yet satisfied. I should now make further offerings to the** ***sharira."*** **He then spoke to the Bodhisattvas and the great disciples, to the gods, the dragons, the** ***yakshas,*** **and so forth in the great assembly, saying, "All of you pay attention and bring your thoughts to one, for I am now going to make offerings to the** ***sharira*** **of the Buddha Virtue Pure and Bright Like the Sun and Moon." Having said that, in front of the eighty-four thousand** ***stupas,*** **as an offering he burned his arms, with their adornments of a hundred blessings, for seventy-two thousand years.**

J2. Burning his arms.

Commentary:

The Bodhisattva All Beings Delight in Seeing then further thought to himself, "Although I have made this offering, my heart is not yet satisfied. Although I burned my body in my last life, I don't feel that I have done all I could. I don't feel I have exhausted my sincerity in making offerings to the Buddha."

We give away a little money and feel that we have created great merit and virtue. This Bodhisattva offered his entire body and still didn't say, "That's enough. I've done my bit. I am number one." The Buddhas of the ten directions had already praised him as foremost, saying, "This is true vigor. This is a true Dharma offering," but he still felt it wasn't enough. This is really a case of "Present as if not there, real as if unreal." He had true merit and virtue, but acted as if he didn't. Basically he had already acquired a tremendous amount of merit and virtue, but he still felt it wasn't very much. The Bodhisattva's resolve is not like that of common people. If we burn off a finger to the Buddha, we remember it our whole lives, thinking no one can compare to us. Bodhisattvas don't think like that.

And so the Bodhisattva All Beings Delight in Seeing decided, **"I should now make further offerings to the *sharira*." He then spoke to the Bodhisattvas and the great disciples, to the gods, the dragons, the *yakshas* and so forth**—the eightfold division—**in the great assembly, saying, "All of you should pay attention and bring your thoughts to one, for I am now going to make offerings to the *sharira* of the Buddha Virtue Pure and Bright Like the Sun and Moon.** Help me by reciting this Buddha's name." **Having said that, in front of the eighty-four thousand** *stupas* he had built for that Buddha, **as an offering he burned his arms, with their adornments of a hundred blessings.** Living beings didn't even have to see his face. Just seeing his arms and hands made all living beings rejoice. Why? He had exquisitely beautiful arms from having made offerings to the Buddha. He burned his arms **for seventy-two thousand years.** They burned for that long. Before, when he burned his body, it burned for twelve hundred years. Why did his arms take so long to burn? This time, his arms belonged to his transformation body, and so he could burn them for any length of time. Seventy-two thousand years is not that long.

Sutra:

> **...thereby causing countless multitudes of hosts seeking to be Hearers and limitless *asamkhyeyas* of people to bring forth the resolve for *anuttarasamyaksambodhi,* and enabling them to dwell in the samadhi of the manifestation of all physical forms.**

J3. Benefits.

Commentary:

Why did he burn his arms, and why for so long? It was just to influence other living beings. Seeing his true mind in making offerings to the Buddha, those living beings who were not true would become true and those who were not sincere would become sincere. In his former life, he burned his entire body; this life he burns his arms. This is no piece of cake, either. It's not easy to do, but he did it anyway, **thereby causing countless multitudes of hosts seeking to be Hearers and limitless *asamkhyeyas* of people to bring forth the resolve for *anuttarasamyaksambodhi.*** In this way he was teaching and transforming living beings **and enabling them to dwell in the samadhi of the manifestation**

of all physical forms, the same samadhi that the Bodhisattva All Beings Delight in Seeing had attained.

Old Master Yinguang had a lot of learning. He lived at Buddha-Peak Mountain on Mount Putuo for eighteen years, during which time he read the Tripitaka over and over. He was extremely reverent when he read the Tripitaka, and he sat up very straight. If he had to go to the bathroom, he would change all of his clothes—everything, even his shoes and socks. Because of his great reverence, he became enlightened. After he got enlightened, he exclusively recited the Buddha's name and established the Lingyan ("Magical Cave") Mountain, a Way-place exclusively for the practice of Buddha recitation, in Suzhou. In that Way-place, people recited the Buddha's name every day. They also had the best food; no other monastery had food like that. So all the monks moved there. They came to recite the Buddha's name and also to "recite" food! Since they ate well, they also recited well. They didn't indulge in idle thinking. If one doesn't eat well, one might have idle thinking. A little good food never hurts.

When this Dharma Master lectured in Nanjing, a funny thing happened. Even though he lectured very well, no one came to listen. There were very few people in that area who understood the Buddhadharma, but he lectured anyway. One night someone showed up. Master Yinguang thought that an audience of one was pretty good. After the lecture he asked the person, "Did you like my lecture? Pretty good, huh?" The man said, "I have no idea what you said."

"Then why are you listening?"

"I'm just waiting to put the chairs away," the man said.

And here he thought he had found someone who "knew his sound"! All of you are ones who know my sound. You listen when I lecture, and so I am really fond of all of you.

Anyway, after that experience, Master Yinguang swore he would never lecture the Sutras in Nanjing again.

One time he was lecturing at the Lay Society in Shanghai, and a female student had a dream. In the dream someone told her, "Hurry up and go to the Lay Society in Shanghai and listen to the *Amitabha Sutra*. Great Strength Bodhisattva is lecturing it there!" This student had no idea who Great Strength Bodhisattva was or what the *Amitabha Sutra* was, but having had this dream, she went there. She spoke to the Old Master, "Actually, I'm not a Buddhist. I had a dream in which someone told me Great Strength Bodhisattva was lecturing the *Amitabha Sutra* at the Lay Society here, so I came. The day after the dream, I saw an ad in the paper, saying that you were lecturing the *Amitabha Sutra* here."

Old Master Yinguang told her, "Don't tell this to anyone. Keep it to yourself."

She had wanted to tell people, but she followed his orders. She also took refuge with him. In less than three years the Old Master entered Nirvana. After he had entered stillness, she told everyone her dream. Everyone then knew that Old Master Yinguang was a transformation of Great Strength Bodhisattva. No one knew at the time. Afterwards, everyone knew. That's how people are. When something is right in front of them, they don't recognize it. When it's gone, they say, "Oh! So that's what it was!" But by then it's too late.

Sutra:

At that time all the Bodhisattvas, gods, humans, *asuras,* and so forth, seeing him without arms, were smitten with grief and said, "The Bodhisattva All Beings Delight in Seeing is our teacher. He has taught and transformed us, but now his arms are burned off and his body deformed."

Then the Bodhisattva All Beings Delight in Seeing made this vow amidst the great assembly, saying, "Having renounced both of my arms, I should certainly attain the Buddha's golden-colored body. If this is true and not false, both of my arms should now be restored to as they were before."

After he had made this vow, his arms were spontaneously restored. This came about through the purity and depth of this Bodhisattva's blessings, virtue, and wisdom.

The three thousand great thousand world system then quaked in six ways. The heavens rained down jeweled flowers, and all the humans and gods gained what they had never had before.

J4. The manifestation of the reward.

Commentary:

At that time all the Bodhisattvas, gods, humans, *asuras,* and so forth, that is, the rest of the eightfold division, **seeing him without arms, were smitten with grief.** The Bodhisattvas got afflicted! They cried **and said, "The Bodhisattva All Beings Delight in Seeing is our teacher. He has taught**

and transformed us so that we could understand the Buddhadharma. **But now his arms are burned off and his body deformed."** Without arms a person looks like a log or something, not very attractive. It was quite a scene, with all the gods, *yakshas*, dragons, *kinnaras*, *garudas*, *gandharvas*, and so on stirring up a big fuss. **Then the Bodhisattva All Beings Delight in Seeing made this vow amidst the great assembly, saying, "Having renounced both of my arms, I should certainly attain the Buddha's golden-colored body. If this is true and not false, both of my arms should now be restored to as they were before.** I should get my two arms back." **After he had made this vow, his arms were spontaneously restored. This came about through the purity and depth of this Bodhisattva's blessings, virtue, and wisdom.** This happened because he had great blessings, wisdom, and virtue. He was also very honest and reliable. He never lied, killed, stole, took intoxicants, or committed sexual misconduct.

The three thousand great thousand world system then quaked in six ways: banging, roaring, cracking, shaking, surging, and rising.

The heavens rained down jeweled flowers, and all the humans and gods gained what they had never had before. They had certainly never seen anything like that before.

Sutra:

> **The Buddha told the Bodhisattva Constellation King Flower, "What do you think? Was the Bodhisattva All Beings Delight in Seeing anyone else? He was just the present Medicine King Bodhisattva. Gifts of his body,**

such as this one, number in the limitless hundreds of thousands of myriads of *kotis* of *nayutas*."

G3. Conclusion—past and present.
H1. Conclusion.

Commentary:

The Buddha, Shakyamuni, **told the Bodhisattva Constellation King Flower, "What do you think? Was the Bodhisattva All Beings Delight in Seeing anyone else? He was just the present Medicine King Bodhisattva. Gifts of his body, such as this one, number in the limitless hundreds of thousands of myriads of *kotis* of *nayutas*."** I have just told you of his burning body and his arms to give you a general idea of how he practiced giving his life for living beings. Actually, his gifts like this one were innumerable.

Sutra:

"Constellation King Flower! If a person who brings forth the resolve desiring to obtain *anuttarasamyaksambodhi* can burn off a finger or a toe as an offering to a Buddha *stupa,* his offering will surpass that of one who uses as offerings countries, cities, wives, and children or even the three thousand great thousand worlds with their mountains, forests, rivers, ponds, and precious objects."

H2. Exhortation to cultivate.

Commentary:

Constellation King Flower! If a person who brings forth the resolve desiring to obtain *anuttarasamyaksambodhi*

can burn off a finger or a toe as an offering to the Buddhas or to **a Buddha *stupa*, his offering will surpass that of one who uses as offerings countries, cities, wives, and children, or even the three thousand great thousand worlds with their mountains, forests, rivers, ponds, and precious objects.**

Sutra:

> **"If, further, a person filled the three thousand great thousand world system with the seven treasures and offered it to the Buddha, to the great Bodhisattvas, Pratyekabuddhas, and Arhats, the merit and virtue that person would obtain would not be equal to that of one who receives and upholds even a single four-line verse of the *Dharma Flower Sutra*, for the latter's blessings are greater by far."**

E2. Praising the Sutra.
F1. Praising the one who upholds it.

Commentary:

If further a person filled the three thousand great thousand world system with the seven treasures and offered it to the Buddha, to the great Bodhisattvas, Pratyekabuddhas, and Arhats, the merit and virtue that person would obtain from making offerings to the Four Kinds of Sages **would not be equal to that of one who receives and upholds even a single four-line verse of the *Dharma Flower Sutra*, for the latter's blessings are greater by far.** The merit and virtue of one who receives and upholds the *Dharma Flower Sutra* greatly exceeds that of one who makes offerings of such precious things.

Sutra:

"Constellation King Flower! Just as, for example, among all the streams, rivers, and bodies of water, the ocean is foremost, so, too, among all the Sutras spoken by the Thus Come One, the *Dharma Flower Sutra* is the deepest and greatest.

"Further, just as among Earth Mountain, Black Mountain, the Lesser Iron Ring Mountain, the Greater Iron Ring Mountain, the Ten Jeweled Mountains, and the entire multitude of mountains, Mount Sumeru is foremost, so, too, among all the Sutras, the *Dharma Flower Sutra* is the most supreme.

"Further, just as among the stars, the Moon God is foremost, so, too, among the thousands of myriads of *kotis* of kinds of Sutra Dharmas, the *Dharma Flower Sutra* shines the brightest.

"Further, just as the Sun God can disperse all darkness, so, too, this Sutra can disperse all the darkness of unwholesomeness.

"Further, just as among the minor kings, the Wheel-Turning Sage King is foremost, so, too, among the Sutras, this Sutra is the most honored.

"Further, just as in the Heaven of the Thirty-three, Lord Shakra is king, so, too, among the Sutras, this Sutra is king.

"Further, just as the great Brahma God is the father of all living beings, so, too, is this Sutra the father of all the worthy sages, those studying, those beyond study, as well as those who have brought forth the Bodhisattva mind.

"Further, just as among the common people, the Srotaapanna, Sakridagamin, Anagamin, Arhat, and Pratyekabuddha are foremost, so, too, among all Sutra Dharmas, whether spoken by the Thus Come Ones, by the Bodhisattvas, or by Hearers, this Sutra is foremost.

"One who can receive and uphold this Sutra, in the same way, is foremost among all living beings.

"Just as among all the Hearers and Pratyekabuddhas, the Bodhisattva is foremost, so, too, among all the Sutra Dharmas, this Sutra is foremost.

"Just as the Buddha is the king of all Dharmas, so, too, is this Sutra the king of all Sutras."

F2. Praising the Dharma that is upheld.
G1. Praising the substance of the Dharma.

Commentary:

Here we have ten analogies. Shakyamuni Buddha calls out again, **Constellation King Flower! Just as, for example, among all the streams, rivers, and bodies of water, the ocean is foremost, so, too, among all the Sutras spoken by the Thus Come One,** the Buddha, **the *Dharma Flower Sutra* is the deepest and greatest.** It's the most wonderful and the most profound.

Further, just as among Earth Mountain, Black Mountain, the Lesser Iron Ring Mountain, the Greater Iron Ring Mountain, the Ten Jeweled Mountains, and the entire multitude of mountains, Mount Sumeru—Wonderfully High Mountain—**is foremost, so, too, among all the Sutras, the *Dharma Flower Sutra* is the most supreme.** The Ten Jeweled Mountains are mentioned in the *Avatamsaka Sutra*.

Further, just as among the stars, the Moon God is foremost, so, too, among the thousands of myriads of *kotis* of kinds of Sutra Dharmas, the *Dharma Flower Sutra* shines the brightest. The other Sutras are like stars, and the *Dharma Flower Sutra* is like the moon, very bright.

Further, just as the Sun God can disperse all darkness, so, too, this Sutra can disperse all the darkness of unwholesomeness. Goodness is light; evil is darkness. The *Dharma Flower Sutra* can break up the darkness of evil.

Further, just as among the minor kings, who are as many as scattered grain, **the Wheel-Turning Sage King,** who rules over four continents, **is foremost, so, too, among the Sutras, this Sutra is the most honored.**

Further, just as in the Heaven of the Thirty-three, Lord Shakra—Lord God—**is king, so, too, among the Sutras, this Sutra is king.**

Further, just as the great Brahma God is the father of all living beings, or so he says, **so, too, is this Sutra the father of all the worthy sages, those studying, those beyond study, as well as those who have brought forth the Bodhisattva mind.**

Most people say they believe in God, meaning the Lord of the Heaven of the Thirty-three. How can the God Brahma claim to be the father of all living beings? At the end of the eon, after the world has gone through the processes of becoming, dwelling, and decay and when it is about to be destroyed and become empty, at that time, some living beings who believe in the Buddha or who cultivate will spontaneously be born in the Second Dhyana Heavens, in the heaven called the Light-Sound Heaven, also known as the Sound Heaven. Then after the period of emptiness has passed and the life span of beings in the Light-Sound Heaven comes to an end and the world is about to be created again, one of the Light-Sound Gods will fall and go to the Great Brahma Heaven. Being just one, single God, friendless and alone, he will wait for some more Light-Sound Gods to fall into the Great Brahma Heaven, some to be the ministers and multitudes of Brahma. Once there's a crowd, the first person who got there and who now calls himself the Great Brahma God, will say, "Hi! You're all here. Guess what? I am the father of all of you!" Actually, this "father" business is purely imaginary. He isn't really their father. Now the text refers to the Great Brahma God as the father of all living beings, but the text is just going along with him here. However, the *Dharma Flower Sutra* is indeed the father of all the Hearers, Pratyekabuddhas, and Bodhisattvas.

Further, just as among the common people, the Srota-apanna, Sakridagamin, Anagamin, Arhat, and Pratyeka-buddha are foremost, so, too, among all Sutra Dharmas, whether spoken by the Thus Come One, by the Bodhi-sattvas, or by the Hearers, this Sutra is foremost.

One who can receive and uphold, read and recite, write out, and bow to **this Sutra** or explain it to others, **in the same way, is foremost among all living beings.**

Just as among all the Hearers and Pratyekabuddhas, the Bodhisattva is foremost, so, too, among all the Sutra Dharmas, this Sutra is foremost.

Just as the Buddha is king of all Dharmas, so, too, is this Sutra the king of all Sutras.

All you Dharma-protecting laymen and laywomen who are associated with the Buddhist Lecture Hall, the Sino-American Buddhist Association, or *Vajra Bodhi Sea:* when you come to the lecture hall, you should concentrate single-mindedly on whatever you came to do, whether it's studying Chinese or English, sitting in meditation, reciting the Buddha's name, or listening to the Sutra lecture. Don't come here and gather in small groups of three, five, or ten people to chat about things that happened eighty thousand eons ago or to make plans for the next eighty thousand eons. People who come to the Buddhist Lecture Hall have to cultivate and not talk so much. The residents shouldn't talk so much with visitors, and visitors shouldn't talk so much with the residents. Your talking obstructs the cultivation of others. If someone is trying to meditate, your talking will cause him to have false thinking; and if you cause a cultivator to have false thinking, you're creating offenses. Unless you have business to take care of, don't engage in casual conversations. If you have legitimate business, you should be able to deal with it in a few brief sentences. You shouldn't have to hold meetings constantly. It's okay to hold a meeting if you have a legitimate reason, but three or five people shouldn't get together just to shoot the breeze. You should know that talking is not as good as reciting the Buddha's name. "Speak one sentence less, and recite the Buddha's name one more time." Recite until your false thoughts die, and then your Dharma body will come to life. Only then can you apply effort successfully. As diligent cultivators, we shouldn't mindlessly chatter. I'm telling you this because some people have told me they don't like to come to the lecture hall because they can't apply effort due to the constant chatter. All of you should pay attention to this and abide by the rules.

Sutra:

> **"Constellation King Flower! This Sutra can save all living beings. This Sutra can lead all living beings to separate from suffering and distress. This Sutra can greatly benefit all living beings, fulfilling their vows. Just as a clear, refreshing pool can quench the thirst of all; as a cold person finds fire; as a naked person finds clothing; as a merchant finds customers; as a child finds its mother; as a passenger finds a boat; as a sick person finds a doctor; as one in a dark place finds a lamp; as a poor person finds a jewel; as the people find a king; as a trader finds the sea; as a torch dispels darkness—the *Dharma Flower Sutra,* in the same way, can cause living beings to leave all suffering and all sickness and pain; it can untie all the bonds of birth and death."**

G2. Praising the function of the Dharma.

Commentary:

Here we have twelve more analogies. Shakyamuni Buddha calls out again, **"Constellation King Flower! This Sutra can save all living beings."** The *Wonderful Dharma Lotus Sutra* has a great function. It can take living beings from great trials and tribulations to happier circumstances. **This Sutra can lead all living beings to separate from suffering and**

distress. This Sutra can greatly benefit all living beings, fulfilling their vows. The great benefits this Sutra brings to living beings cannot be expressed in words. Whatever wish or vow living beings have, they can fulfill it. It's **just as a clear, refreshing pool can quench the thirst of all.**

It is **as a cold person finds a fire.** Not understanding the Buddhadharma is like being cold. Understanding the Buddhadharma is like being warmed by a fire.

It is **as a naked person finds clothing.** Before you read the *Dharma Flower Sutra*, you were as if naked. Now, studying the *Dharma Flower Sutra* and understanding it is like getting some clothes.

It is **as a merchant finds customers,** so that he can do business.

It is **as a child finds its mother.** Reading and reciting the *Dharma Flower Sutra*, you have found your Dharma-body mother.

It is **as a passenger finds a boat.** To get across the sea, you need a boat. The *Dharma Flower Sutra* is a great boat.

It is **as a sick person finds a doctor.** Otherwise he can't get well. If a sick person finds a good doctor, he can get well. We are like sick people and the *Dharma Flower Sutra* is a great doctor who can cure us.

It is **as one in a dark place finds a lamp.** In a dark room, you can't see anything. If you light a lamp, then you can see everything. The *Dharma Flower Sutra* is just a bright light in a dark room.

It is **as a poor person finds a jewel.** It's also like a poor man who finds a treasure, the seven treasures of gold, silver, lapis lazuli, crystal, mother of pearl, red pearls, and carnelian.

It is **as the people find a king.** If the citizens don't have a king, there is chaos. Now they have a king.

It is **as a trader finds the sea.** A trader is a person who wanders around selling his wares. Traders gain their treasures traveling on the sea.

It is **as a torch dispels darkness. The *Dharma Flower Sutra,* in the same way** as the twelve analogies just mentioned, **can cause living beings to leave all suffering and all sickness and pain. It can untie all the bonds of birth and death.** Birth and death is like a rope that ties us up. Now, reading and reciting the *Dharma Flower Sutra,* we can untie those knots and obtain freedom and liberation.

Sutra:

> **"If a person hears the *Dharma Flower Sutra,* writes it out himself, or employs others to write it out, the limits of the merit and virtue he shall obtain cannot be calculated even by means of the Buddha's wisdom.**
>
> **"If a person writes out this Sutra and makes offerings to it of flowers; incense; beads; burning incense; powdered incense; paste incense; banners and canopies; clothing; and lamps of various kinds such as butter lamps, oil lamps and fragrant oil lamps, lamps of *champaka* oil, lamps of *sumana* oil, lamps of *patala* oil, lamps of *varshika* oil, and lamps of *navamalika* oil, the merit and virtue obtained is also limitless."**

F3. Showing the depth of blessings of one who upholds the Sutra.
G1. The blessings of one who upholds the entire Sutra.

Commentary:

If a person hears the *Dharma Flower Sutra*—if he has good roots and good causal conditions enabling him to hear the *Wonderful Lotus Flower Sutra*—and if he **writes it out himself, or employs others to write it out, the limits of the merit and virtue he shall obtain cannot be calculated even by means of the Buddha's wisdom.** Using the Buddha's omniscient wisdom to try to figure out how much merit and virtue he has, one still could not find its limits.

If a person writes out this Sutra and makes offerings to it of flowers; incense; beads; burning incense; powdered incense; paste incense; banners and canopies; clothing; and lamps of various kinds such as butter lamps, oil lamps, fragrant oil lamps, lamps of *champaka* oil, lamps of *sumana* oil, lamps of *patala* oil, lamps of *varshika* oil, and lamps of *navamalika* oil, the merit and virtue obtained is also limitless. "*Patala*" is the name of a "flower that blooms repeatedly." "*Varshika*" are "flowers that bloom in the summer." "*Navamalika*" means "variegated flowers"; they have patches of all different colors.

Sutra:

> **"Constellation King Flower, if a person hears this chapter, "The Past Deeds of Medicine King Bodhisattva," he will also obtain limitless, boundless merit and virtue. If a woman hears this chapter, "The Past Deeds of Medicine King Bodhisattva," and is able to receive and uphold it, after quitting this woman's body, she will not undergo one again. If, after the passing of the Thus Come One, in the last five hundred years, there is a woman who, hearing this Sutra, can cultivate according to its teachings, at the end of her present life, she will go straight to the**

blissful world of the Buddha Amitayus, where she is surrounded by great Bodhisattvas. Born from a lotus flower, seated on a jeweled seat, this person will never again be tormented by desire, tormented by hate and stupidity, or tormented by the filth of arrogance and jealousy. He will obtain the Bodhisattva's spiritual penetrations and the patience with the nonproduction of dharmas. Having obtained this patience, his eye will be pure. By means of this pure eye, he will see Buddhas, Thus Come Ones, equal in number to the grains of sand in seven million two thousands *kotis* of *nayutas* of Ganges Rivers.

"At that time all the Buddhas will praise this person from afar saying, 'Good indeed, good indeed, good man, that within the Dharma of Shakyamuni Buddha you can receive, uphold, read, recite, and ponder this Sutra, and speak it for others. The merit and virtue you obtain is limitless and boundless. Fire cannot burn it. Water cannot flood it. Your merit and virtue is such that if a thousand Buddhas spoke of it together, they could not exhaust it.

"'You have already been able to destroy the thieves of Mara, to ruin the troops of birth and death, and to demolish all remaining enemies.

"'Good man, a hundred thousand Buddhas, with their power of spiritual penetrations, all protect you. In all the world with its gods and humans, there is none like you, with the exception of the Thus Come One. The Hearers and Pratyekabuddhas, and even the Bodhisattvas, cannot equal you in wisdom and Dhyana concentration.'

"Constellation King Flower, such is the power of the merit and virtue and wisdom accomplished by this Bodhisattva.

"If a person hears this chapter, "The Past Deeds of Medicine King Bodhisattva," and rejoices in accord, praising its goodness, that person's mouth in his present life will always emit the fragrance of a blue lotus. The pores of his body will always emit the perfume of oxhead *chandana*. The merit and virtue he obtains will be as described above."

G2. The blessings of one who upholds this chapter.
H1. The description.

Commentary:

Constellation King Flower, if a person hears this chapter, "The Past Deeds of Medicine King Bodhisattva,"—not even the entire *Dharma Flower Sutra,* but just this chapter alone—**he will also obtain limitless, boundless merit and virtue.**

If a woman hears this chapter, "The Past Deeds of Medicine King Bodhisattva," and is able to receive and uphold it, read and recite it, **after quitting this woman's body, she will not undergo one again.** Thinking it a lot of trouble and affliction, she doesn't want to be a woman. Then after her life as a woman naturally comes to an end—this doesn't mean that she commits suicide because she doesn't want to be a woman, but rather that her life naturally comes to an end—having undergone her retribution, she will not undergo a woman's body again. If she receives and upholds this chapter, then after her life as a woman comes to a natural end, she won't have to be a woman again. If you want to be a woman, even though it's trouble, and you don't want to be a man, then you can do as you please. No one is going to force you to give it up. It's up to you. So women hearing this shouldn't be afraid and think they aren't going to be women, run off, and not listen to the Sutra.

If, after the passing of the Thus Come One, in the last five hundred years, there is a woman who, hearing this Sutra or this chapter, **can cultivate according to its teachings**—cultivating patience, compassion, and the emptiness of dharmas, these three Dharma-doors—**at the end of her present life she will go straight to the blissful world of the Buddha Amitayus, where she is surrounded by great Bodhisattvas.** The Pure Ocean-wide Assembly of Bodhisattvas surround the Buddha as he speaks the Dharma. They are mindful of the Buddha, mindful of the Dharma, and mindful of the Sangha. **Born from a lotus flower, seated on a jeweled seat**—seated on a golden terrace, with a lotus flower for a father and mother—**this person will never again be tormented by desire.** So you see, the Buddha really understands the thoughts of living beings. He knows that women have a difficult time seeing through greed and desire. These two words can totally confuse even the most intelligent women. Desire is extremely fierce. One may crave for food and always think, "What tasty thing can I have to eat?" With thoughts like this, eventually one goes to steal food—off to the refrigerator to see what's good and to steal some. One can also be greedy for nice clothing. "I think I need a new outfit." One can also be greedy for a fancy house to live in. Everyone has greedy thoughts like these about food, clothing, and a place to live.

There is another kind of desire that is even fiercer than

the desire for food, clothing, and a place to live. This is a desire that comes with you at birth. Right when you are born, you come with these impure thoughts. The desire for food, clothing, or a place to live is a small problem compared with this one. This biggest problems of all is sexual desire. These thoughts are difficult indeed to stop. But if you can stop them, then you are on your way to becoming a sage, an Arhat, or a Bodhisattva. If you aren't a sage, an Arhat, or a Bodhisattva, you won't be able to stop thoughts of sexual lust. You won't have control over yourself. You will be tormented by such thoughts. Then, confused by lust, without rhyme or reason, you will get angry.

Moreover, this person who upholds the *Dharma Flower Sutra* will not be **tormented by hate and stupidity.** Because you are hateful, you become stupid, totally lacking wisdom. One is afflicted by hatred and stupidity, but the root of the problem is sexual desire. Hatred and stupidity follow in its wake. Further, one won't be **tormented by the filth of arrogance and jealousy.** If you understand the *Dharma Flower Sutra* you won't be arrogant and think yourself higher than Mount Sumeru. You won't look down on everyone. Jealousy means you are afraid someone else is going to be better than you. You should know that arrogance and jealousy are filth; they are unclean, extremely dirty. Why haven't you become enlightened? Why do you lack wisdom? It's just because you are arrogant and jealous. Here, we are talking about women, but men are subject to these faults, too. If you have such faults, you should change them. Hearing this chapter about Medicine King, you should put down your body. You should think, "Medicine King Bodhisattva burned his body and his arms as an offering to the Buddha. What have I got to be so arrogant about?" Get rid of your arrogance. When it's gone, you will obtain purity and give rise to genuine wisdom. Giving rise to genuine wisdom, you won't be tormented by greed and desire, by hatred, stupidity, and jealousy and all those impure thoughts.

He will obtain the Bodhisattva's spiritual penetrations and the patience with the nonproduction of dharmas. Having obtained this patience, his eye will be pure. One who reads and recites this chapter, "The Past Deeds of Medicine King Bodhisattva," will not be defiled and will obtain the Bodhisattva's spiritual penetrations. The patience with the nonproduction of dharmas means that one doesn't see the slightest dharma produced or the slightest dharma destroyed. One experiences such a state and endures it mentally. Having obtained this patience, your eye will be pure and will obtain the merit and virtues enumerated above.

By means of this pure eye, he will see the Buddhas of the ten directions. Why can't we see them? Because our eyes aren't pure. If your eyes obtain purity, then you can see **Buddhas, Thus Come Ones, equal in number to the grains of sand in seven million, two thousand *kotis* of *nayutas* of Ganges Rivers.**

At that time all the Buddhas will praise this person from afar, saying, "Good indeed, good indeed, good man, that within the Dharma of Shakyamuni Buddha, you can receive, uphold, read, recite, and ponder this Sutra, and speak it for others. The merit and virtue you obtain is limitless and boundless. You understand the Sutra's doctrines yourself, and you can communicate those doctrines to others. In general, **fire cannot burn it.** And if you enter a fire yourself, you won't burn. But you can't try this out to see if it works. If you try it out, you're going to burn. It has to be an accident. Let's say you are in the mountains: The mountain may catch on fire, but you won't get burned. If your house catches on fire accidentally, the fire won't burn you. If you set the fire yourself trying to run an experiment, the Buddhas aren't going to pay any attention to you. **Water cannot flood it.** You won't drown in any body of water—seas, rivers, lakes, or ponds. **Your merit and virtue is such that if a thousand Buddhas spoke of it together, they could not exhaust it.** If a thousand Buddhas all together tried to speak about your merit and virtue, they would never finish.

You have already been able to destroy the thieves of Mara—the demons of afflictions, the demons of the mind, all the demons—and **to ruin the troops of birth and death.** There is no more birth and death for you. **And to demolish all remaining enemies**, having totally vanquished them.

Good man, a hundred thousand Buddhas, with their power of spiritual penetrations, all protect you. The Buddhas are mindful and protective of you. **In all the world with its gods and humans, there is none like you.** No one has as much merit and virtue, **with the exception of the Thus Come One.** Of course the Buddha's merit is greater than yours. **The Hearers and Pratyekabuddhas, and even the Bodhisattvas, cannot equal you in wisdom and Dhyana concentration.** Even their accomplishments do not come up to yours.

Constellation King Flower, such is the power of the merit and virtue and wisdom accomplished by this Bodhisattva who receives and upholds, reads and recites, explains and writes out the *Dharma Flower Sutra*.

If a person hears this chapter, "The Past Deeds of Medicine King Bodhisattva"—he doesn't need to hear the whole Sutra, just this chapter—**and** if he **rejoices in accord, praising its goodness, that person's mouth in his present life will always emit the fragrance of a blue lotus. From the pores of his body he will always emit the perfume of oxhead** *chandana*—a very sweet incense. **The merit and virtue he obtains will be as described above.**

Sutra:

"Therefore, Constellation King Flower, I entrust to you this chapter, "The Past Deeds of Medicine King Bodhisattva." After my passing, in the last five hundred years, propagate it extensively in Jambudvipa. Do not let it become extinct, thereby allowing evil demons, demonic denizens, all the heavenly dragons, *yakshas, kumbhandas,* and so forth to get their way.

"Constellation King Flower, you should use the power of spiritual penetrations to protect this Sutra. Why? Because this Sutra is good medicine for the sicknesses of those in Jambudvipa. If a sick person gets to hear this Sutra, his sickness will be cured immediately. He will not grow old or die.

"Constellation King Flower, if you see a person who receives and upholds this Sutra, you should scatter blue lotuses filled with powdered incense over him as an offering. Having done that, you should reflect: 'Before long, this person will certainly lay out a grass mat, sit in the Way-place, vanquish the troops of Mara, blow the Dharma conch, strike the great Dharma drum, and save all living beings from the sea of old

age, sickness, and death. Therefore, when those who seek the Buddha Way see one who receives and upholds this Sutra, they should bring forth a reverent heart in this way."

H2. The entrustment.

Commentary:

"Therefore, Constellation King Flower, I entrust to you this chapter, 'The Past Deeds of Medicine King Bodhisattva'. I am putting you in charge of distributing this very important chapter, so bring forth your resolve to do so. **After my passing, in the last five hundred years** of the Dharma-ending Age, **propagate it extensively in Jambudvipa,** distribute and circulate it. **Do not let it become extinct,** be cut off, **thereby allowing evil demons, demonic denizens, all the heavenly dragons, *yakshas, kumbhandas,* and so forth, to get their way,** to run around and do whatever they wish." "*Kumbhanda*" means "wintermelon ghost" and also "nightmare ghost." Aside from *kumbhandhas,* there are other kinds of ghosts like the *putana,* the *kalaputana,* and all the rest. Most people think ghosts just come in one variety, but they come in myriads of varieties. All living beings come in many varieties. Take ants, for example. There are many, many different kinds: yellow, white, black, big, small, long, short, and so forth. Who knows how many different kinds of ants there are? Some are very, very tiny. There are also black, yellow, red, green mosquitoes—all kinds of them. Such little things! Butterflies also come in infinite varieties.

There are just as many varieties of spirits and ghosts.

This applies to all the various species of living beings. You could never classify them all. They vary from country to country. In cold climates the ants are different from the ones in hot climates. Western ants are not the same as Eastern ants.

Constellation King Flower, you should use the power of spiritual penetrations to protect this Sutra. Why? Because this Sutra is good medicine for the sicknesses of people in Jambudvipa. The chapter "The Past Deeds of Medicine King Bodhisattva" is good medicine for sick people here. **If a sick person gets to hear this Sutra,** if he recites this chapter of the Sutra, **his sickness will be cured immediately. He will not grow old or die.** Isn't this wonderful?

"But I've never seen anyone in the world who didn't get old just because they recited this chapter," you say.

How many people do you know? Just because you haven't met any people who do not grow old or die, you can't say they don't exist.

Constellation King Flower, if you see a person who receives and upholds this Sutra, and this chapter, **you should scatter blue lotuses filled with powdered incense over him as an offering.** Take a blue lotus, fill it with powdered incense, and then sprinkle it over the one who recites this chapter of the *Dharma Flower Sutra*. **Having done that, you should reflect: "Before long, this person will certainly lay out a grass mat**—a seat made of auspicious grass—**sit in the Way-place** beneath the Bodhi tree, and accomplish Buddhahood. He will **vanquish the troops of Mara, blow the Dharma conch,** and **strike the great Dharma drum.** When you blow the Dharma conch, all the demons are afraid. **And** he will **save all living beings from the sea of old age, sickness, and death. Therefore, when those who seek the Buddha Way see one who receives and upholds this Ṣutra, they should bring forth a reverent heart in this way.** They should be very reverent and respectful.

Sutra:

> **When this chapter, "The Past Deeds of Medicine King Bodhisattva," was spoken, eighty-four thousand Bodhisattvas obtained the *dharani* of understanding the speech of all living beings.**

D3. The benefits.

Commentary:

When this chapter, "The Past Deeds of Medicine King Bodhisattva," was spoken by Shakyamuni Buddha, **eighty-four thousand Bodhisattvas obtained the *dharani* of understanding the speech of all living beings.** This is the language of samadhi. They knew the languages of all living beings.

Sutra:

> **From within the jeweled *stupa*, the Thus Come One Many Jewels praised Constellation King Flower Bodhisattva, saying, "Good indeed, good indeed, Constellation King Flower! You have accomplished such inconceivable merit and virtue that you are able to question Shakyamuni Buddha about matters such as these and to benefit limitless living beings."**

D4. Praise from Many Jewels Thus Come One.

Commentary:

From within the jeweled *stupa*, the Thus Come One Many Jewels praised Constellation King Flower Bodhisattva, saying, "Good indeed, good indeed, Constellation King Flower! You have accomplished such inconceivable merit and virtue this time. It can't be conceived of by the mind or expressed in words. It is excellent **that you are able to question Shakyamuni Buddha about matters such as these and benefit limitless living beings.** This is of infinite benefit to all living beings, entirely inexpressible and inconceivable in its magnitude."

End of Chapter Twenty-three

At that time the Bodhisattva Mahasattva Wondrous Sound, having made offerings to Shakyamuni Buddha and to the *stupa* of the Buddha Many Jewels, returned to his own country.

The Wonderful Dharma Lotus Flower Sutra

Chapter Twenty-four: The Bodhisattva Wondrous Sound

Sutra:

AT THAT TIME Shakyamuni Buddha emitted a light from his flesh cowl, the mark of a great person, and a radiance issued forth from the white hair-mark between his eyebrows, everywhere illumining Buddha worlds to the east equal in number to the grains of sand in one hundred and eight myriads of *kotis* of *nayutas* of Ganges Rivers.

Beyond these, there was a world by the name of Adorned with Pure Light. In that world was a Buddha by the name of Wisdom of Pure Flower Constellation King Thus Come One, One Worthy of Offerings, One of Right and Universal Knowledge, One Whose Clarity and Conduct Are Complete, Well Gone One Who Understands the World, Supreme Lord, Regulating Hero, Teacher of Gods and Humans, Buddha, World Honored One. He was reverently surrounded by a great multitude of limitless, boundless Bodhisattvas to whom he was speaking the Dharma.

The light that issued forth from Shakyamuni Buddha's white hair-mark universally illumined that country.

At that time in the country Adorned with All Pure Light, there was a Bodhisattva by the name of Wondrous Sound, who had, for a long time, planted the roots of virtue by making offerings and drawing near to limitless hundreds of thousands of myriads of *kotis* of Buddhas and had completely accomplished profound wisdom.

He had obtained the Samadhi of the Wonderful Banner Mark,

the Samadhi of the Dharma Flower,

the Samadhi of Pure Virtue,

the Samadhi of the Playfulness of Constellation King,

the Samadhi of No Affinity,

the Samadhi of the Seal of Wisdom,

the Samadhi of Understanding the Speech of all Living Beings,

the Samadhi of the Accumulation of All Merit and Virtue,

the Samadhi of Purity,

the Samadhi of Playful Roaming of Spiritual Penetrations,

the Samadhi of the Wisdom Torch,

the Samadhi of Royal Splendor,

the Samadhi of Pure Light,

the Samadhi of the Pure Treasury,

the Samadhi of Difference, and

the Samadhi of Sun-Revolution.

He obtained such great samadhis as these, equal in number to the grains of sand in a hundred thousand myriad *kotis* of Ganges Rivers.

When Shakyamuni Buddha's light illumined his body, he immediately spoke to the Buddha Wisdom of Pure Flower Constellation King, saying, "World Honored One, I should go to the Saha world to bow to, draw near to, and make offerings to Shakyamuni Buddha, and to see the Dharma Prince Bodhisattva Manjushri, the Bodhisattva Medicine King, the Bodhisattva Courageous Giving, the Bodhisattva Constellation King Flower, the Bodhisattva Mind of Superior Practice, the Bodhisattva King of Adornment, and the Bodhisattva Medicine Superior."

At that time the Buddha Wisdom of Pure Flower Constellation King told the Bodhisattva Wondrous Sound, "You should not look lightly upon that country or think of it as inferior. Good man, the Saha world is uneven, its earth, stones, and mountains are filled with filth and evil. The Buddha's body is lowly and small. The Bodhisattvas are also small in shape. Your body is forty-two thousand *yojanas* in height. My body is six hundred and eighty myriad *yojanas* in height. Your body is superb and upright, with a hundred thousand myriad blessings and fine and subtle light. Therefore, if you go, do not look lightly upon that country, its Buddha, Bodhisattvas, or lands."

The Bodhisattva Wondrous Sound said to the Buddha, "World Honored One, I shall now go to the Saha world, and this is all through the power of the Thus Come One; the playful roaming spiritual penetrations of the Thus Come One; and the adornments of merit, virtue, and wisdom of the Thus Come One."

Then the Bodhisattva Wondrous Sound, without rising from his seat, his body motionless, entered samadhi. With the power of samadhi he went to Mount Gridhrakuta, not far from the Dharma seat. He then created by transformation eighty-four thousand jeweled lotuses, their stems of Jambunada gold, their leaves of silver, their pistils of *vajra,* and their sepals of *kumshuka* jewels.

The Dharma Prince Manjushri, seeing the lotuses, asked the Buddha, "World Honored One, what is the reason for this portent, these several thousands of myriads of lotuses, their stems of Jambunada gold, their leaves of silver, their pistils of *vajra* and their sepals of *kumshuka*?"

At that time Shakyamuni Buddha told Manjushri, "The Bodhisattva Mahasattva Wondrous Sound, surrounded by eighty-four thousand Bodhisattvas, wishes to come from the country of the Buddha Wisdom of Pure Light Constellation King to this Saha world to make offerings, draw near to, and bow to me. He also wishes to make offerings and listen to the *Dharma Flower Sutra.*"

Manjushri said to the Buddha, "World Honored One, what good roots has this Bodhisattva planted, what merit and virtue has he cultivated that he can have this great power of spiritual penetrations? What samadhi has he practiced? I pray that you will tell us the name of this samadhi. We, too wish to cultivate it diligently, for by practicing this samadhi we will be able to see this Bodhisattva, his appearance, size, and awesome manner, and his comings and goings. We only pray that the World Honored One will, by means of the power of spiritual penetrations, let us see that Bodhisattva when he comes."

At that time Shakyamuni Buddha told Manjushri, "The Thus Come One Many Jewels who passed into stillness long ago shall, for your sakes, manifest these signs."

The Buddha Many Jewels then said to the Bodhisattva, "Good man, come here! The Dharma Prince Manjushri wishes to see you in person."

The Bodhisattva Wondrous Sound then disappeared from his own country, and together with eighty-four thousand Bodhisattvas, set out on his way. The countries they passed through quaked in six ways, and all rained down lotuses made of the seven treasures, while a hundred thousand kinds of heavenly music played spontaneously.

The Bodhisattva's eyes were like the broad, large petals of a blue lotus. A hundred thousand myriad moons combined would not surpass the awesome beauty of his facial features. His body was the color of gold, adorned with limitless hundreds of thousands of meritorious virtues. The light of his awesome virtue blazed with brilliant splendor, and his marks were all perfect. His body was as solid as that of Narayana. He entered a terrace made of the seven treasures, and rose up into space to the height of seven *tala* trees. With Bodhisattvas reverently surrounding him, he came to Mount Gridhrakuta in the Saha world.

Having arrived, he stepped down from the terrace of seven treasures. Taking a necklace of beads, its value in the hundreds of thousands, he went before Shakyamuni Buddha, bowed with his head at the Buddha's feet, offered up the necklace and said to the Buddha, "World Honored One, the Buddha Wisdom of Pure Flower Constellation King inquires after the World Honored One. Are you free from sickness and worry? Are you energetic in your comings and goings? Is your practice peaceful and happy? Are the four elements in harmony? Are you enduring the affairs of the world? Are living beings easy to save, without much greed, hatred, stupidity, jealousy, stinginess, or arrogance? None are not filial in their behavior toward their parents, are they, or disrespectful toward Shramanas, deviant in their views, unwholesome in their thoughts, or not in control of the five emotions? World Honored One, have living beings been able to conquer the hateful demons? Has the long since passed Thus Come One Many Jewels, within the jeweled *stupa,* come to hear the Dharma?

"He also wishes to inquire as to whether the Thus Come One Many Jewels is peaceful and secure, free from worry, and long abiding in the world 'Worthy of Being Endured.'"

"World Honored One, we now wish to see the Buddha Many Jewels. We only pray that the World Honored One will allow us to see him."

Shakyamuni Buddha told the Buddha Many Jewels, "The Bodhisattva Wondrous Sound wishes to see you."

The Buddha Many Jewels spoke to Wondrous Sound, saying, "Good indeed! Good indeed, that in order to make offerings to Shakyamuni Buddha and to hear the *Dharma Flower Sutra,* as well as to see Manjushri and the others, you have come here."

The Bodhisattva Flower Virtue then spoke to the Buddha, saying, "World Honored One, what good roots has the Bodhisattva Wondrous Sound planted, and what meritorious virtues has he cultivated that he has these spiritual powers?"

The Buddha told the Bodhisattva Flower Virtue, "In the past there was a Buddha by the name of Clouds and Thunder Sound King, Thus Come One, Arhat, Samyaksambuddha. His country was called Manifesting All Worlds. His eon was named Delightful to See. For twelve thousand years, the Bodhisattva Wondrous Sound made offerings to the Buddha Clouds and Thunder Sound King of a hundred thousand kinds of music. He also offered up eighty-four thousand bowls made of the seven treasures. As a result of these deeds, he has been born in the country of the Buddha Wisdom of Pure Flower Constellation King and now possesses these spiritual powers.

"Flower Virtue, what do you think? Could the Bodhisattva Wondrous Sound who made offerings of music and jeweled vessels to the Buddha Clouds and Thunder Sound King have been anyone else? He was just this Bodhisattva Mahasattva Wondrous Sound.

"Flower Virtue! The Bodhisattva Wondrous Sound has in the past made offerings and drawn near to limitless Buddhas, for a long time planting the roots of virtue and encountering hundreds of thousands of myriads of *kotis* of *nayutas* of Buddhas equal in number to the sands of the Ganges.

"Flower Virtue, you see merely the body of the Bodhisattva Wondrous Sound as it appears here. However, this Bodhisattva manifests all kinds of bodies and speaks this Sutra in many places for living beings.

"He may manifest in the body of a Brahma King; he may manifest in the body of Shakra; he may manifest in the body of the God of Sovereignty; he may manifest in the body of the God of Great Sovereignty; he may manifest in the body of a great heavenly general; he may manifest in the body of the heavenly king Vaishravana; he may manifest in the body of a wheel-turning sage king;

he may manifest in the body of a minor king; he may manifest in the body of an elder; he may manifest in the body of a layperson; he may manifest in the body of a minister of state; he may manifest in the body of a Brahman; he may manifest in the body of a Bhikshu, Bhikshuni, Upasaka, or Upasika; he may manifest in the body of an elder's wife or a layman's wife; he may manifest in the body of a minister's wife; he may manifest in the body of a Brahman's wife; he may manifest in the body of a young boy or a young girl. He may manifest in the body of a god, dragon, *yaksha, gandharva, asura, garuda, kinnara, mahoraga,* a human, or a nonhuman and speak this Sutra.

"He can rescue all in the hells, the hungry ghosts, and the animals, as well as those in difficulty. He can even transform himself into a woman of the king's inner court and speak this Sutra.

"Flower Virtue, the Bodhisattva Wondrous Sound can rescue all living beings in the Saha world. The Bodhisattva Wondrous Sound can, in this way, transform into all these different kinds of bodies and speak this Sutra for living beings in the Saha world and still lose nothing of his spiritual penetrations, transformations, and wisdom.

"This Bodhisattva's wisdom shines brightly upon the Saha world, causing living beings to each gain understanding. In worlds like Ganges' sands throughout the ten directions, he does the same.

"To those who must be crossed over by the form of a Hearer, he manifests in the form of a Hearer and speaks the Dharma for them.

"To those who must be crossed over by the form of a

Pratyekabuddha, he manifests in the form of a Pratyekabuddha and speaks the Dharma for them.

"To those who must be crossed over by the form of a Bodhisattva, he manifests in the form of a Bodhisattva and speaks the Dharma for them.

"To those who must be crossed over by the form of a Buddha, he manifests in the form of a Buddha and speaks the Dharma for them. In this way he manifests in all manner of forms to cross them over in the appropriate manner, even to the point of manifesting entering stillness to those who must be crossed over by manifesting entering stillness.

"Flower Virtue, such is the great power of the spiritual penetrations and wisdom of the Bodhisattva Mahasattva Wondrous Sound."

At that time the Bodhisattva Flower Virtue said to the Buddha, "World Honored One, the Bodhisattva Wondrous Sound has deeply planted the roots of goodness. World Honored One, in what samadhi does this Bodhisattva dwell that he is able in this way to transform himself and save living beings?"

The Buddha told the Bodhisattva Flower Virtue, "Good man, this samadhi is called the Manifestation of All Physical Forms. The Bodhisattva Wondrous Sound, dwelling in this samadhi, can in this way benefit limitless living beings."

When this chapter on the Bodhisattva Wondrous Sound had been spoken, those who had accompanied the Bodhisattva Wondrous Sound, eighty-four thousand in all, all obtained the Samadhi of the Manifestation of all Physical Forms. Limitless Bodhisattvas in the Saha world also gained this samadhi, as well as *dharani*.

At that time the Bodhisattva Mahasattva Wondrous Sound, having made offerings to Shakyamuni Buddha and to the *stupa* of the Buddha Many Jewels, returned to his own country. The countries he passed through quaked in six ways, precious lotus flowers rained down, and hundreds of thousands of myriads of *kotis* of kinds of music played. When he arrived at his own country, surrounded by the eighty-four thousand Bodhisattvas, he went before the Buddha Wisdom of Pure Flower Constellation King and said, "World Honored One, I have been to the Saha world where I benefited living beings. I saw Shakyamuni Buddha and the *stupa* of Many Jewels Buddha, bowed, and made offerings to them. I also saw the Bodhisattva Manjushri, the Dharma Prince, as well as the Bodhisattva Medicine King, the Bodhisattva Who Has Gained the Power of Diligent Vigor, the Bodhisattva Courageous Giving, and others, and enabled eighty-four thousand Bodhisattvas to obtain the Samadhi of the Manifestation of All Physical Forms."

When this chapter on the comings and goings of the Bodhisattva Wondrous Sound had been spoken, forty-two thousand gods obtained the patience with the Non-production of Dharmas. The Bodhisattva Flower Virtue obtained the Dharma Flower Samadhi.

Chapter Twenty-four: The Bodhisattva Wondrous Sound

A Simple Explanation by the Venerable Master Hsuan Hua

Sutra:

AT THAT TIME Shakyamuni Buddha emitted a light from his flesh cowl, the mark of a great person, and a radiance issued forth from the white hair-mark between his eyebrows, everywhere illumining Buddha worlds to the east equal in number to the grains of sand in one hundred and eight myriads of *kotis* of *nayutas* of Ganges Rivers.

Beyond these, there was a world by the name of Adorned with Pure Light. In that world was a Buddha by the name of Wisdom of Pure Flower Constellation King Thus Come One, One Worthy of Offerings, One of Right and Universal Knowledge, One Whose Clarity and Conduct Are Complete, Well Gone One Who Understands the World, Supreme Lord, Regulating Hero, Teacher of Gods and Humans, Buddha, World Honored One. He was reverently surrounded by a great multitude of limitless, boundless Bodhisattvas to whom he was speaking the Dharma.

The light that issued forth from Shakyamuni Buddha's white hair-mark universally illumined that country.

C2. Disciples who receive the Dharma.
D1. The chapter "Wondrous Sound."
E1. Emitting light to summon those from the east.

Commentary:

This is **Chapter Twenty-four, "The Bodhisattva Wondrous Sound."** This Bodhisattva's sound was subtle, wonderful, and inconceivable. Why was it wonderful? When he spoke the Dharma, his voice remained forever in the ears of living beings. Living beings whose ears received this amazing sound would never forget the Dharma that Wondrous Sound Bodhisattva had taught them.

At that time Shakyamuni Buddha emitted a light from his flesh cowl, the mark of a great person. The flesh cowl represents the perfection of the fruit of enlightenment. The mark of a great person refers to the Buddha's thirty-two marks. The flesh cowl is one of those marks. **And a radiance issued forth from the white hair-mark between his eyebrows.** The white hair-mark light represents the perfect cause of the Middle Way. The cause and fruit are both perfect and nondual. The fruit is just the cause; the cause is just the fruit. This doctrine represents the Middle Way.

This light was **everywhere illumining Buddha worlds to the east equal in number to the grains of sand in one hundred and eight myriads of *kotis* of *nayutas* of Ganges Rivers.**

Beyond these, there was a world by the name of Adorned with Pure Light. In that world was a Buddha by

the name of Wisdom of Pure Flower Constellation King. The "Pure Flower" is the lotus. The "Constellation King" refers to the moon, because the moon is the king of the stars. "Wisdom" means that he had wisdom like the moon, which shines on all things. **Thus Come One, One Worthy of Offerings, One of Right and Universal Knowledge, One Whose Clarity and Conduct Are Complete, Well Gone One Who Understands the World, Supreme Lord, Regulating Hero, Teacher of Gods and Humans, Buddha, World Honored One. He was reverently surrounded by a great multitude of limitless, boundless Bodhisattvas to whom he was speaking the Dharma.** This Buddha was speaking the Dharma for all the great Bodhisattvas, great Arhats, great Bhikshus, great Bhikshunis, great novices, and so on.

The light that issued forth from Shakyamuni Buddha's white hair-mark universally illumined that country.

Sutra:

> **At that time in the country Adorned with All Pure Light, there was a Bodhisattva by the name of Wondrous Sound, who had, for a long time, planted the roots of virtue by making offerings and drawing near to limitless hundreds of thousands of myriads of *kotis* of Buddhas and had completely accomplished profound wisdom.**
>
> **He had obtained the Samadhi of the Wonderful Banner Mark,**
> **the Samadhi of the Dharma Flower,**
> **the Samadhi of Pure Virtue,**
> **the Samadhi of the Playfulness of Constellation King,**
> **the Samadhi of No Affinity,**

the Samadhi of the Seal of Wisdom,

the Samadhi of Understanding the Speech of all Living Beings,

the Samadhi of the Accumulation of All Merit and Virtue,

the Samadhi of Purity,

the Samadhi of Playful Roaming of Spiritual Penetrations,

the Samadhi of the Wisdom Torch,

the Samadhi of Royal Splendor,

the Samadhi of Pure Light,

the Samadhi of the Pure Treasury,

the Samadhi of Difference, and

the Samadhi of Sun-Revolution.

He obtained such great samadhis as these, equal in number to the grains of sand in a hundred thousand myriad *kotis* of Ganges Rivers.

E2. Coming westward on command.
F1. The reason for coming.
G1. Narrator describes his virtue.

Commentary:

This passage of text lists sixteen samadhis. These sixteen are chosen to represent the limitless great samadhis. It's not easy to explain sixteen samadhis. It would be even harder to explain more than sixteen!

At that time in the country Adorned with All Pure Light, there was a Bodhisattva by the name of Wondrous Sound. We say in the East there is Wondrous Sound and in the West there is Contemplator of the World's Sounds. People who don't understand the Buddhadharma sometimes insist that they are Dharma brothers, but really they are far apart. It's ten myriad *kotis* of Buddhalands from here to the West. It's one hundred and eight myriad *kotis* of *nayutas* of Buddhalands of Ganges Rivers' sands from here to the East. That's really too far away. I don't believe that they could be brothers, maybe "blood-brothers," but not real brothers.

Wondrous Sound was a Bodhisattva **who had, for a long time, planted the roots of virtue.** A long time doesn't mean one or two days, one or two months, or one or two years. It means millions of years. When you study the Buddhadharma, you shouldn't think that two and a half days is enough. You should persevere in your study.

He spent his time **by making offerings and drawing near to limitless hundreds of thousands of myriads of *kotis* of Buddhas and had completely accomplished profound wisdom.** He had realized the profound wisdom.

He had obtained the Samadhi of the Wonderful Banner Mark. The Wonderful Banner Mark is the real mark. The basic substance of the real mark is higher than all things. Although it is higher than all things, it is without a mark. Although it is without a mark, there's nothing not marked by it. There is no mark and nothing not marked, and so we call it the Wonderful Banner Mark Samadhi.

The Samadhi of the Dharma Flower. The Dharma Flower Samadhi is the nonduality of cause and effect. The cause is just the effect; the effect is just the cause. Cause and effect are simultaneous.

Why is the analogy made to the lotus flower? The lotus flower blooms and bears fruit at the same time. As soon as the lotus blooms, the lotus seeds are present as well.

This also represents the nonduality of provisional and real. One bestows the provisional for the sake of the real, and opens the provisional to reveal the real. The provisional is just the real; the real is just the provisional. The provisional and real are not two, they are nondual. Cause and effect are not two. The roots and traces are not two. That is, the roots, the events of the distant past, and the traces now manifesting are not two. The present life is the traces; past lives are the roots. They are not two. This is the Dharma Flower Samadhi.

The Samadhi of Pure Virtue. What is pure virtue? It is to separate from the filth of the three kinds of delusion: view and thought delusions, delusions of ignorance, and delusions like dust and sand. Delusions just make you confused. When you see a state, you get confused. When you think about a state, you get confused. When you can neither see nor think clearly, you have the delusion of ignorance.

View delusion means that "faced with a state, you give rise to greed and love." Something happens and you get greedy and produce craving for it.

Thought delusion refers to "producing discrimination based on faulty understanding of principle." You are confused about the principle, and you discriminate about it. The more you discriminate, the farther off you get; the farther off you get, the more you discriminate. You become separated from your original wisdom by a great distance.

Delusion of ignorance refers to those things you don't understand. You don't know why, but you get mad. You don't know why, but you do crazy things. You don't know why, but you take drugs. These things are all done out of ignorance. It's said,

Ignorance and its various aspects
Are the root of pain.

The three delusions are impure, so they are called filth. When one separates from the filth of the three delusions and is certified to the original pure self-nature, that is called the Samadhi of Pure Virtue.

The Samadhi of the Playfulness of Constellation King. This samadhi is just like a play, a game. The parts get handed out, and you take your place on the stage for the play, or you sit in the audience. It represents provisional wisdom. You use your provisional expedient wisdom to act out your part in the play. With provisional wisdom you illuminate potentials. You must have provisional wisdom to attract the opportune living beings. If you try to use real wisdom, it won't work. Real wisdom illumines principle, not potential beings. Illumining the potential beings is like the moon, which waxes and wanes. It waxes when it's supposed to wax, and wanes when it's supposed to wane. It takes a clever, ingenious kind of wisdom to do these things. If you aren't clever and ingenious but are rather dull and plodding, then it's not going to suit the potentials. Dull and plodding, you might go and get angry at the poor people. You try to lecture Dharma to these people, but instead you get enraged. Lecturing the Dharma should be a happy event. Even if you are debating with someone, you can be cordial about it. You don't have to get mad and be a sore loser. That just shows you lack provisional wisdom. To say nothing of provisional wisdom, you don't have any sense at all! If you listen to someone speak the Dharma and it doesn't suit you and you get mad, it's a sign that you lack provisional wisdom.

The Samadhi of No Affinity. If you get mad, then you really have no affinities or wisdom! "No affinity" refers to the equality of great kindness. It means treating all people with equal kindness, whether or not you have affinities with them. This is called

Great kindness for those with whom one has no affinities
Great compassion of being of the same substance with all.

The Samadhi of the Seal of Wisdom. The seal of wisdom refers to the three types of wisdom in a single thought. With one thought the three types of wisdom exist: All-Wisdom, the Wisdom of Modes of the Way, and the Wisdom of All Modes. These three types of wisdom are used to "seal" and "certify" all dharmas.

The Samadhi of Understanding the Speech of All Living Beings. In this samadhi you unite with all living beings. You understand the languages not only of people, but of all creatures: horses, cows, sheep, chickens, dogs, pigs —all of them. Not only do you understand the languages of one country, but you understand the languages of all people and creatures in all worlds. You understand the languages of all living beings within the nine Dharma realms. One language is all languages; all languages are one language. With the understanding of one, all are understood. But first you have to understand the one. If you don't understand the one, you can't understand them all. Confucius' disciple Yan Yuan could hear one principle and understand ten. Zi Gong could hear one principle and understand two. All languages are dharmas born of causes and conditions. Within the dharmas born of causes and conditions, one understands that they do not go beyond emptiness, falseness, and the middle. Understanding the contemplation of emptiness, falseness, and the middle, you then gain the Samadhi of Understanding the Speech of All Living Beings.

The Samadhi of the Accumulation of All Merit and Virtue. While dwelling in one samadhi, one perfects the merit and virtue of all samadhis. One samadhi penetrates all samadhis. The merit and virtue of all samadhis returns to the one samadhi.

The Samadhi of Purity. Purity refers to the purification of the six sense faculties: eyes, ears, nose, tongue, body, and mind. When the six sense faculties are purified, one attains to the comfort of mutual interpenetration of the six faculties.

The Samadhi of Playful Roaming of Spiritual Penetrations. Spiritual penetrations are the wonderful function of comfort. One uses comfortable spiritual penetrations to teach and transform living beings as one roams and plays throughout the three thousand great thousand world system. It's like an illusion, like putting on a play. Yesterday I brought up the analogy of the world being like a play, and all of you understood it right away. Actually, the play I was talking about was not like the one you understood it to be. I'm talking about the play of the playful roaming samadhi, a kind of spiritual penetration. To act in this play, you must have spiritual powers. This is the samadhi of illusion. One takes an illusory journey among people, gathering in and saving all living beings. You employ the spiritual powers of all things being like an illusion.

The Samadhi of the Wisdom Torch. Wisdom is like a torch, a kind of light. Using the wisdom of great equality, one universally illumines all darkness, dispersing it entirely.

The Samadhi of Royal Splendor. This means to adorn the royal nature. The self-nature is like a king. To adorn it, you must cultivate. Basically, the self-nature is complete with the myriad virtues, and it is entirely unobstructed and interpenetrating. You very casually take up one dharma with which you can connect with all dharmas. Whichever dharma you select has the Dharma nature.

The Samadhi of Pure Light. This refers to the three types of wisdom: All-Wisdom, Wisdom of Modes of the Way, and the Wisdom of All Modes. These three types of wisdom are perfect and pure, illumining all dharmas without exception.

The Samadhi of the Pure Treasury. In a single thought, the mind obtains purity and can universally gather in the myriad virtues.

The Samadhi of Difference. "Different" means different from the Three Vehicles: the Hearers, Those Enlightened to Conditions, and Bodhisattvas. The Samadhi of Difference is the Buddha's samadhi.

And the Samadhi of Sun-Revolution. One uses real wisdom to illumine the principle, shining on the universe. Like the sun moving through the sky, one doesn't dwell anywhere.

He obtained such great samadhis as these, equal in number to the grains of sand in a hundred thousand myriad *kotis* of Ganges Rivers. The Bodhisattva Wondrous Sound, in the past, made offerings of music to all the Buddhas, and so he obtained the aforementioned sixteen great samadhis. Actually, he didn't obtain just sixteen samadhis, but as many samadhis as there are grains of sand in a hundred thousand myriad *kotis* of Ganges Rivers.

Sutra:

When Shakyamuni Buddha's light illumined his body, he immediately spoke to the Buddha Wisdom of Pure Flower Constellation King, saying, "World Honored One, I should go to the Saha world to bow to, draw near to, and make offerings to Shakyamuni Buddha, and to see the Dharma Prince Bodhisattva Manjushri, the Bodhisattva Medicine King, the Bodhisattva Courageous Giving, the Bodhisattva Constellation King Flower, the Bodhisattva Mind of Superior Practice, the Bodhisattva King of Adornment, and the Bodhisattva Medicine Superior."

G2. Having been illumined, he takes leave of the Buddha.

Commentary:

From the white hair-mark between his eyebrows, Shakyamuni Buddha had emitted light that illuminated the eastern direction, shining into lands as many as the grains of sand in one hundred and eight myriad *kotis* of *nayutas* of Ganges Rivers. It shone on the Bodhisattva Wondrous Sound in the world Pure Adornment.

When Shakyamuni Buddha's light illumined his body, he immediately spoke to the Buddha Wisdom of Pure Flower Constellation King, saying, "World Honored One, having received the light of Shakyamuni Buddha, I feel **I should go to the Saha world to bow to, draw near to, and make offerings to Shakyamuni Buddha, and to see the Dharma Prince Bodhisattva Manjushri, the Bodhisattva Medicine King, the Bodhisattva Courageous Giving, the Bodhisattva Constellation King Flower, the Bodhisattva**

Mind of Superior Practice, the Bodhisattva King of Adornment, and the Bodhisattva Medicine Superior."

Sutra:

> **At that time the Buddha Wisdom of Pure Flower Constellation King told the Bodhisattva Wondrous Sound, "You should not look lightly upon that country or think of it as inferior. Good man, the Saha world is uneven, its earth, stones, and mountains are filled with filth and evil. The Buddha's body is lowly and small. The Bodhisattvas are also small in shape. Your body is forty-two thousand *yojanas* in height. My body is six hundred and eighty myriad *yojanas* in height. Your body is superb and upright, with a hundred thousand myriad blessings and fine and subtle light. Therefore, if you go, do not look lightly upon that country, its Buddha, Bodhisattvas, or lands."**

G3. Instructions from that Buddha.

Commentary:

At that time the Buddha Wisdom of Pure Flower Constellation King told the Bodhisattva Wondrous Sound, "You should not look lightly upon that country or think of it as inferior. You shouldn't do a lot of negative thinking about its bad qualities. **Good man, the Saha world is uneven. Its earth, stones, and mountains are filled with filth and evil. That Buddha's body is lowly and small,** about six feet tall, quite short and tiny. **The Bodhisattvas are also small in shape**—there are many mini-Bodhisattvas.

"Your body is forty-two thousand *yojanas* in height. The living beings there will stand at your feet, look up at you, and won't even be able to see your head! **My body is six hundred and eighty myriad *yojanas* in height. Your body is superb and upright, with a hundred thousand myriad blessings and fine and subtle light.** When you get to the Saha world you will tower over Shakyamuni Buddha with all your glorious appearance. **Therefore, if you go, do not look lightly upon that country, its Buddha, Bodhisattvas, or lands."** This was the advice that the Buddha gave the Bodhisattva Wondrous Sound.

Actually, Wondrous Sound Bodhisattva wouldn't look down on the beings of the Saha world, so why did the Buddha Wisdom of Pure Flower Constellation King give him this advice? Some of the Bodhisattvas who went along with him belonged to the provisional vehicle and lacked a certain amount of wisdom. Since their wisdom wasn't as profound, he was afraid they might look down on the Saha world, and having done so, fall.

Sutra:

> **The Bodhisattva Wondrous Sound said to the Buddha, "World Honored One, I shall now go to the Saha world, and this is all through the power of the Thus Come One; the playful roaming spiritual penetrations of the Thus Come One; and the adornments of merit, virtue, and wisdom of the Thus Come One."**

G4. The Bodhisattva takes advice.

Commentary:

The Bodhisattva Wondrous Sound said to the Buddha, "World Honored One, I shall now go to the Saha world,

and this is all through the power of the Thus Come One. It is not on my own power, but rather by means of **the playful roaming spiritual penetrations of the Thus Come One and the adornments of merit, virtue, and wisdom of the Thus Come One."**

The Bodhisattva Wondrous Sound could have gone on his own. Why did he give credit to the Buddha? It was because he yielded all merits to the Buddha. He wouldn't say, "See how talented I am? I can go to the Saha world. My spiritual powers and miraculous functions are inconceivable." Instead, he said, "The Buddha's helping me. That's how I can do it." Western people would say he was being too polite, or that perhaps he really didn't have such spiritual powers, but that's not the case. He did have the powers, but he wished to show his respect for the Buddha in this way, and so he credited everything to the Buddha's compassionate assistance. It was through the Buddha's compassion and patience, and the merit of the emptiness of dharmas.

Sutra:

> **Then the Bodhisattva Wondrous Sound, without rising from his seat, his body motionless, entered samadhi. With the power of samadhi he went to Mount Gridhrakuta, not far from the Dharma seat. He then created by transformation eighty-four thousand jeweled lotuses, their stems of Jambunada gold, their leaves of silver, their pistils of *vajra,* and their sepals of *kumshuka* jewels.**

G5. Manifesting signs in advance of his arrival.
H1. Sending the lotuses on ahead.

Commentary:

Then the Bodhisattva Wondrous Sound, without rising from his seat, his body motionless in full lotus posture, his mind without false thinking, **entered samadhi. With the power of samadhi he went to Mount Gridhrakuta,** to the Dharma assembly at Vulture Peak, **not far from the Dharma seat** of Shakyamuni Buddha. **He then created by transformation eighty-four thousand jeweled lotuses, their stems of Jambunada gold, their leaves of silver, their pistils of *vajra,* and their sepals of *kumshuka* jewels.** *Kumshuka* is a Sanskrit word that means "red jewelled flower."

Sutra:

> **The Dharma Prince Manjushri, seeing the lotuses, asked the Buddha, "World Honored One, what is the reason for this portent, these several thousands of myriads of lotuses, their stems of Jambunada gold, their leaves of silver, their pistils of *vajra* and their sepals of *kumshuka*?"**

H2. Manjushri's question.

Commentary:

The Dharma Prince Manjushri, seeing the lotuses, asked the Buddha, "World Honored One, what is the reason for this portent, these several thousands of myriads of lotuses, their stems of Jambunada gold, their leaves of silver, their pistils of *vajra* and their sepals of *kumshuka*?" Although he had such great spiritual powers, Manjushri still did not understand this state. Even though the Bodhisattvas were all Equal Enlightenment Bodhisattvas and had been certified to the same fruition, still each one had his special abilities. If one manifested some spiritual powers, the other might not understand them, and vice versa. Wondrous Sound Bodhisattva manifested this portent. Manjushri, even though he really did understand, asked the question on behalf of the others who didn't.

Sutra:

> **At that time Shakyamuni Buddha told Manjushri, "The Bodhisattva Mahasattva Wondrous Sound, surrounded by eighty-four thousand Bodhisattvas, wishes to come from the country of the Buddha Wisdom of Pure Light Constellation King to this Saha world to make offerings, draw near to, and bow to me. He also wishes to make offerings and listen to the *Dharma Flower Sutra.*"**

H3. Shakyamuni Buddha's answer.

Commentary:

At that time Shakyamuni Buddha told Manjushri, "The Bodhisattva Mahasattva Wondrous Sound, surrounded by eighty-four thousand Bodhisattvas, wishes to come from the country of the Buddha Wisdom of Pure Light Constellation King to this Saha world to make offerings, draw near to, and bow to me. He also wishes to make offerings and listen to the *Dharma Flower Sutra.*" Those are the reasons for his coming to this world.

Sutra:

> **Manjushri said to the Buddha, "World Honored One, what good roots has this Bodhisattva planted, what**

merit and virtue has he cultivated that he can have this great power of spiritual penetrations? What samadhi has he practiced? I pray that you will tell us the name of this samadhi. We, too wish to cultivate it diligently, for by practicing this samadhi we will be able to see this Bodhisattva, his appearance, size, and awesome manner, and his comings and goings. We only pray that the World Honored One will, by means of the power of spiritual penetrations, let us see that Bodhisattva when he comes."

H4. Manjushri asks to see him.

Commentary:

Manjushri said to the Buddha, "World Honored One, what good roots has this Bodhisattva planted? What good roots did he plant in the past? **What merit and virtue has he cultivated that he can have this great power of spiritual penetrations?** And **what samadhi has he practiced** to gain such fine spiritual powers? **I pray that you will tell us the name of this samadhi. We, too, wish to cultivate it diligently.** All of us here in the Dharma assembly, the Hearers and the Bodhisattvas, also want to cultivate this samadhi and to obtain such inconceivably great spiritual penetrations. **For by practicing this samadhi, we will be able to see this Bodhisattva.** Once we accomplish this samadhi, we will become this Bodhisattva's fellow cultivators; we will have cultivated the same Dharma-door. And then we will be able to see this Bodhisattva, **his appearance, size, and awesome manner, and his comings and goings,** in the four comportments of walking, standing, sitting, and lying down. **We only pray that the World Honored One will, by means of the power of spiritual penetrations, let us see that Bodhisattva when he comes.** I, Manjushri, and all the other Bodhisattvas, Bhikshus, Bhikshunis, Upasakas, Upasikas, and so forth all want to see him."

Sutra:

> **At that time Shakyamuni Buddha told Manjushri, "The Thus Come One Many Jewels who passed into stillness long ago shall, for your sakes, manifest these signs."**

H5. Shakyamuni Buddha gives the job to Many Jewels.

Commentary:

Manjushri Bodhisattva wanted to see the Bodhisattva Wondrous Sound and asked the Buddha to invite him to the assembly. **At that time Shakyamuni Buddha told Manjushri, "The Thus Come One Many Jewels who passed into stillness long ago,** who went to Nirvana long ago, **shall, for your sakes, manifest these signs."**

Sutra:

> **The Buddha Many Jewels then said to the Bodhisattva, "Good man, come here! The Dharma Prince Manjushri wishes to see you in person."**

H6. Many Jewels orders him to the assembly.

Commentary:

The Buddha Many Jewels then spoke up and **said to the Bodhisattva** Wondrous Sound, **"Good man, come here! The**

Dharma Prince Manjushri wishes to see you in person. He wants to make friends with you."

Sutra:

> **The Bodhisattva Wondrous Sound then disappeared from his own country, and together with eighty-four thousand Bodhisattvas, set out on his way. The countries they passed through quaked in six ways, and all rained down lotuses made of the seven treasures, while a hundred thousand kinds of heavenly music played spontaneously.**

F2. Their trip.
G1. On the road with his retinue.

Commentary:

The Bodhisattva Wondrous Sound then disappeared from his own country. Right after the Buddha Many Jewels gave his order, the Bodhisattva suddenly disappeared from his own country, Adorned with Pure Light, **and together with eighty-four thousand Bodhisattvas, set out on his way.** They all took off for the Saha world for a vacation. They were a rather large group. They didn't charter a plane, however, they came via spiritual powers. **The countries they passed through quaked in six ways, and all rained down lotuses made of the seven treasures.** Wherever they went, flowers rained down out of the sky, **while a hundred thousand kinds of heavenly music played spontaneously.** As they flew through space, they were accompanied by heavenly music. Nobody had to play it, either; it played all by itself.

Sutra:

The Bodhisattva's eyes were like the broad, large petals of a blue lotus. A hundred thousand myriad moons combined would not surpass the awesome beauty of his facial features. His body was the color of gold, adorned with limitless hundreds of thousands of meritorious virtues. The light of his awesome virtue blazed with brilliant splendor, and his marks were all perfect. His body was as solid as that of Narayana. He entered a terrace made of the seven treasures and rose up into space to the height of seven *tala* trees. With Bodhisattvas reverently circumambulating him, he came to Mount Gridhrakuta in the Saha world.

G2. His appearance as he ascended the terrace.

Commentary:

The Bodhisattva's eyes were like the broad, large petals of a blue lotus. A hundred thousand myriad moons combined would not surpass the awesome beauty of his facial features. His body was the color of gold, adorned with limitless hundreds of thousands of meritorious virtues. The light of his awesome virtue blazed with brilliant splendor. Anyone who saw him automatically became very reverent. They were afraid, and yet they wanted to draw near him, because he had awesome virtue and he was also good and compassionate. **And his marks were all perfect. His body was as solid as that of Narayana**—perfect and indestructible in all respects. The Buddha has eighty subsidiary characteristics. Well, this Bodhisattva had at least seventy-nine.

Narayana refers to the Vajra Power Knight whose body is as solid as *vajra*. He's not afraid of anything—atom bombs, hydrogen bombs, nothing. There's no way to harm him.

He entered a terrace made of the seven treasures and rose up into space to the height of seven *tala* trees, about fifty feet. **With Bodhisattvas reverently circumambulating him, he came to Mount Gridhrakuta in this Saha world,** to Magic Vulture Mountain in the Saha world.

Sutra:

> **Having arrived, he stepped down from the terrace of seven treasures. Taking a necklace of beads, its value in the hundreds of thousands, he went before Shakyamuni Buddha, bowed with his head at the Buddha's feet, offered up the necklace and said to the Buddha, "World Honored One, the Buddha Wisdom of Pure Flower Constellation King inquires after the World Honored One. Are you free from sickness and worry? Are you energetic in your comings and goings? Is your practice peaceful and happy? Are the four elements in harmony? Are you enduring the affairs of the world? Are living beings easy to save, without much greed, hatred, stupidity, jealousy, stinginess, or arrogance? None are not filial in their behavior toward their parents, are they, or disrespectful toward Shramanas, deviant in their views, unwholesome in their thoughts, or not in control of the five emotions? World Honored One, have living beings been able to conquer the hateful demons? Has the long since passed Thus Come One Many Jewels, within the jeweled *stupa,* come to hear the Dharma?**

"He also wishes to inquire as to whether the Thus Come One Many Jewels is peaceful and secure, free from worry, and long abiding in the world 'Worthy of Being Endured.'"

G3. Making inquiries.

Commentary:

Having arrived, he stepped down from the terrace of seven treasures. Taking a necklace of beads, its value in the hundreds of thousands of pieces of gold, **he went before Shakyamuni Buddha, bowed with his head at the Buddha's feet, and offered up the necklace** as an offering to Shakyamuni Buddha, **and said to the Buddha, "World Honored One, the Buddha Wisdom of Pure Flower Constellation King inquires after the World Honored One.** My teacher asked me to inquire after Shakyamuni Buddha. He wants to know, **are you free from sickness and worry?** You are not sick, are you? **Are you energetic in your comings and goings?** When you rise and when you rest, are you sprightly? **Is your practice peaceful and happy? Are the four elements in harmony?** Earth, air, fire, and water—are they regulated properly?" When people are sick we say that their four elements are out of harmony. One may get too much fire, and the fire overcomes the water. Or one may get too much air, which overcomes the earth; or too much earth, which stops up the water. If, within one's body, the four elements are regulated, then one will not be sick.

"Are you enduring the affairs of the world? Is it bearable? **Are living beings easy to save, without much greed, hatred, stupidity, jealousy, stinginess, or arrogance? None are not filial in their behavior toward their parents,**

are they? Or disrespectful toward Shramanas—left-home people? They're not **deviant in their views, or unwholesome in their thoughts,** are they? They aren't stupid, are they? They have given rise to wisdom, right? Aren't living beings very clear now? Haven't they turned their backs on the dust to unite with enlightenment? They will wake up real soon, won't they?"

If you aren't filial to your parents, you won't be able to cultivate. If you can't cultivate, you can't become a Buddha. If you aren't filial to your parents, why would you listen to the Buddhadharma? Filiality is the most basic of doctrines. It's important not to be at odds with your parents or to treat them badly. Shramanas are left-home people. They diligently cultivate precepts, samadhi, and wisdom and put to rest greed, hatred, and stupidity. Shramanas are worthy of respect. To look upon them as ordinary people is a mistake. Shramanas are the Sangha jewel. No matter whether they cultivate or not, you should be respectful toward them. You can't think, "Oh, he's left-home, but he's just like me. Look how greedy he is, how hateful and stupid! He can't even talk, let alone do anything! Why should I respect him? He's not even as good as me! In fact, it seems right that he should bow to me!" If you aren't respectful toward Shramanas, you won't be able to enter the Way and cultivate. If you don't even respect the Triple Jewel, how can you cultivate? If you get mad at left-home people thinking, "Bald-headed freaks! They just eat, sleep, and wear clothes, and do nothing else!" you are having "deviant views" and "unwholesome thoughts." To think that left-home people aren't different from laypeople is a deviant view; it is unwholesome.

"Or they are **not in control of the five emotions,** are they?" Basically, people have seven emotions: happiness, anger, grief, fear, love, hatred, and desire. "The five emotions" refers to happiness, anger, love, hatred, and desire. It is not easy to control these five emotions. Living beings are basically controlled by their emotions and follow their desires, thinking they are free. That's a mistake.

"World Honored One, have living beings been able to conquer the hateful demons—the demons of death, the demons of sickness, the demons of afflictions, the demons of one's own mind, and heavenly demons? **Has the long since passed Thus Come One Many Jewels, within the jeweled *stupa*, come to hear the Dharma?"** Why did the Bodhisattva Wondrous Sound ask this question? He already saw that the Thus Come One Many Jewels was there. However, he wasn't asking on his own behalf. He was representing the Buddha Wisdom of Pure Flower Constellation King in making these courteous inquiries.

"He, the Bodhisattva Wisdom of Pure Flower Constellation King, **also wishes to inquire as to whether the Thus Come One Many Jewels is peaceful and secure, free from worry, and long abiding in the world 'Worthy of Being Endured'."** The Buddha Many Jewels vowed that wherever the *Dharma Flower Sutra* was being lectured, he would manifest his jeweled *stupa* in space to certify the speaking of the Sutra.

Sutra:

> **"World Honored One, we now wish to see the Buddha Many Jewels. We only pray that the World Honored One will allow us to see him."**

G4. Asking to see Many Jewels.

Commentary:

"World Honored One, we now wish to see the Buddha Many Jewels." The Bodhisattva Wondrous Sound asked Shakyamuni Buddha, **"We only pray that the World Honored One will allow us to see him.** Please be compassionate and let us see him."

Sutra:

> **Shakyamuni Buddha told the Buddha Many Jewels, "The Bodhisattva Wondrous Sound wishes to see you."**
>
> **The Buddha Many Jewels spoke to Wondrous Sound, saying, "Good indeed! Good indeed, that in order to make offerings to Shakyamuni Buddha and to hear the *Dharma Flower Sutra,* as well as to see Manjushri and the others, you have come here."**
>
> **The Bodhisattva Flower Virtue then spoke to the Buddha, saying, "World Honored One, what good roots has the Bodhisattva Wondrous Sound planted, and what meritorious virtues has he cultivated that he has these spiritual powers?"**

G5. Shakyamuni passes the message.
G6. Praise from within the *stupa*.
G7. Questions and answers about past causes.
H1. The question.

Commentary:

Shakyamuni Buddha told the Buddha Many Jewels, "The Bodhisattva Wondrous Sound wishes to see you."

The Buddha Many Jewels spoke to Wondrous Sound, saying, "Good indeed! Good indeed, that in order to

make offerings to Shakyamuni Buddha and to hear the *Dharma Flower Sutra,* as well as to see Manjushri Bodhisattva, Medicine King Bodhisattva, **and the others, you have come here."**

The Bodhisattva named **Flower Virtue then spoke to the Buddha, saying, "World Honored One, what good roots has the Bodhisattva Wondrous Sound planted** in the distant past, **and what meritorious virtues has he cultivated that he has these spiritual powers?"**

Sutra:

The Buddha told the Bodhisattva Flower Virtue, "In the past there was a Buddha by the name of Clouds and Thunder Sound King, Thus Come One, Arhat, Samyaksambuddha. His country was called Manifesting All Worlds. His eon was named Delightful to See. For twelve thousand years, the Bodhisattva Wondrous Sound made offerings to the Buddha Clouds and Thunder Sound King of a hundred thousand kinds of music. He also offered up eighty-four thousand bowls made of the seven treasures. As a result of these deeds, he has been born in the country of the Buddha Wisdom of Pure Flower Constellation King and now possesses these spiritual powers.

"Flower Virtue, what do you think? Could the Bodhisattva Wondrous Sound who made offerings of music and jeweled vessels to the Buddha Clouds and Thunder Sound King have been anyone else? He was just this Bodhisattva Mahasattva Wondrous Sound.

"Flower Virtue! The Bodhisattva Wondrous Sound has in the past made offerings and drawn near to

limitless Buddhas, for a long time planting the roots of virtue and encountering hundreds of thousands of myriads of *kotis* of *nayutas* of Buddhas equal in number to the sands of the Ganges.

H2. The answer.

Commentary:

The Buddha told the Bodhisattva Flower Virtue, "In the past there was a Buddha by the name of Clouds and Thunder Sound King Thus Come One, Arhat, One Worthy of Offerings, **Samyaksambuddha,** One of Right and Universal Knowledge. **His country was called Manifesting All Worlds. His eon was named Delightful to See. For twelve thousands years, the Bodhisattva Wondrous Sound made offerings to the Buddha Clouds and Thunder Sound King of a hundred thousand kinds of music,** and so he obtained a wondrous sound. This is like when we sing praises and chants in front of the Buddha. In the future, we, too, can obtain a wondrous sound.

He also offered up eighty-four thousand bowls made of the seven treasures. As a result of these deeds, he has been born in the country of the Buddha Wisdom of Pure Flower Constellation King and now possesses these great **spiritual powers.**

Flower Virtue, what do you think? Could the Bodhisattva Wondrous Sound who made offerings of music and jeweled vessels to the Buddha Clouds and Thunder Sound King have been anyone else? He was just this Bodhisattva Mahasattva Wondrous Sound present right here in the Dharma assembly.

Flower Virtue, the Bodhisattva Wondrous Sound has in the past made offerings and drawn near to limitless Buddhas, for a long time planting the roots of virtue and encountering hundreds of thousands of myriads of *kotis* of *nayutas* of Buddhas equal in number to the sands of the Ganges, and so now he has such great spiritual powers.

Sutra:

"Flower Virtue, you see merely the body of the Bodhisattva Wondrous Sound as it appears here. However, this Bodhisattva manifests all kinds of bodies and speaks this Sutra in many places for living beings.

"He may manifest in the body of a Brahma King; he may manifest in the body of Shakra; he may manifest in the body of the God of Sovereignty; he may manifest in the body of the God of Great Sovereignty; he may manifest in the body of a great heavenly general; he may manifest in the body of the heavenly king Vaishravana; he may manifest in the body of a wheel-turning sage king; he may manifest in the body of a minor king; he may manifest in the body of an elder; he may manifest in the body of a layperson; he may manifest in the body of a minister of state; he may manifest in the body of a Brahman; he may manifest in the body of a Bhikshu, Bhikshuni, Upasaka, or Upasika; he may manifest in the body of an elder's wife or a layman's wife; he may manifest in the body of a minister's wife; he may manifest in the body of a Brahman's wife; he may manifest in the body of a young boy or a young girl. He may manifest in the body of a god, dragon, *yaksha, gandharva, asura,*

garuda, kinnara, mahoraga, a human, or a nonhuman and speak this Sutra.

"He can rescue all in the hells, the hungry ghosts, and the animals, as well as those in difficulty. He can even transform himself into a woman of the king's inner court and speak this Sutra.

"Flower Virtue, the Bodhisattva Wondrous Sound can rescue all living beings in the Saha world. The Bodhisattva Wondrous Sound can, in this way, transform into all these different kinds of bodies and speak this Sutra for living beings in the Saha world and still lose nothing of his spiritual penetrations, transformations, and wisdom.

"This Bodhisattva's wisdom shines brightly upon the Saha world, causing living beings to each gain understanding. In worlds like Ganges' sands throughout the ten directions, he does the same.

"To those who must be crossed over by the form of a Hearer, he manifests in the form of a Hearer and speaks the Dharma for them.

"To those who must be crossed over by the form of a Pratyekabuddha, he manifests in the form of a Pratyekabuddha and speaks the Dharma for them.

"To those who must be crossed over by the form of a Bodhisattva, he manifests in the form of a Bodhisattva and speaks the Dharma for them.

"To those who must be crossed over by the form of a Buddha, he manifests in the form of a Buddha and speaks the Dharma for them. In this way he manifests in all manner of forms to cross them over in the appropriate manner, even to the point of manifesting

entering stillness to those who must be crossed over by manifesting entering stillness.

"Flower Virtue, such is the great power of the spiritual penetrations and wisdom of the Bodhisattva Mahasattva Wondrous Sound."

E3. Propagating the Sutra in the ten directions.
F1. The manifestation in different forms to speak the Dharma.

Commentary:

"Flower Virtue, you see merely the body of the Bodhisattva Wondrous Sound as it appears here. However, this Bodhisattva manifests in all kinds of bodies and speaks this Sutra in many places for living beings. He is not just here in our Dharma assembly. He speaks the *Dharma Flower Sutra* in many, many places for living beings.

He may manifest in the body of a Brahma King and speak the Dharma. **He may manifest in the body of Shakra,** otherwise known as the God of Christianity, also called Lord God. He is the lord of the Heaven of the Thirty-three.

He may manifest in the body of the God of Sovereignty; he may manifest in the body of the God of Great Sovereignty; he may manifest in the body of a great heavenly general; he may manifest in the body of the heavenly king Vaishravana. Vaishravana is one of the four heavenly kings. He governs the heaven in the north; his name means "much learning." **He may manifest in the body of a wheel-turning sage king. He may manifest in the body of a minor king,** one of the many kings "scattered like grain," to teach living beings. **He may manifest in the body of a** noble and wealthy **elder,** someone with great blessings and virtue. **He may manifest in the body of a layperson. He**

may manifest in the body of a minister of state; he may manifest in the body of a Brahman, one who cultivates pure conduct. **He may manifest in the body of a** great **Bhikshu,** a great **Bhikshuni,** a great **Upasaka, or** a great **Upasika** to teach and transform living beings.

He may manifest in the body of an elder's wife or a layman's wife; he may manifest in the body of a minister's wife; he may manifest in the body of a Brahman's wife; he may manifest in the body of a young boy or a young girl, to teach and transform living beings.

He may manifest in the body of a god, dragon, ***yaksha, gandharva, asura, garuda, kinnara, mahoraga***—members of the eightfold division—or **a human or a nonhuman, and speak this Sutra,** the *Dharma Flower Sutra*.

He can rescue all in the hells, the hungry ghosts, and the animals—those in the three evil paths—**as well as those in difficulty,** that is, those experiencing the eight difficulties. **He can even transform himself into a woman of the king's inner court and speak this Sutra.**

Flower Virtue, the Bodhisattva Wondrous Sound can rescue all living beings in the Saha world. The Bodhisattva Wondrous Sound can, in this way, transform into all these different kinds of bodies and speak this Sutra for living beings in the Saha world and still lose nothing of his spiritual penetrations, transformations, and wisdom. As he manifests a body, his spiritual penetrations and wisdom don't decrease. They remain exactly the same.

This Bodhisattva's wisdom shines brightly upon the Saha world with various wisdom lights **causing living beings each to gain understanding** of the Buddhadharma according to his abilities. **In worlds like Ganges' sands**

throughout the ten directions, he does the same. Not only in the Saha world, but in all worlds, he appears in all their different bodies.

To those who must be crossed over by the form of a Hearer, he manifests in the form of a Hearer and speaks the Dharma of the Four Truths **for them.** He appears as one of the Small Vehicle.

To those who must be crossed over by the form of a Pratyekabuddha, he manifests in the form of a Pratyekabuddha and speaks the Dharma of the Twelve Causes and Conditions **for them.**

To those who must be crossed over by the form of a Bodhisattva, he manifests in the form of a Bodhisattva and speaks the Dharma of the Six Perfections and the myriad conducts **for them.**

To those who must be crossed over by the form of a Buddha, he manifests in the form of a Buddha and speaks the Dharma for them. In this way he manifests in all manner of forms to cross them over in the appropriate manner, even to the point of manifesting entering stillness, the mark of Nirvana, **to those who must be crossed over by manifesting entering stillness.**

Flower Virtue, such is the great power of the spiritual penetrations and wisdom of the Bodhisattva Mahasattva Wondrous Sound.

The Winter Chan Session begins on November 15th and will last for fourteen weeks. The best thing would be if no one spoke, but instead just applied effort single-mindedly. When you're sitting, don't make any noise. Keep quiet and peaceful. Don't use beads to recite the Buddha's name, or make any other kind of sounds. Let us hope that during the session everyone can become enlightened. If you make noise, it disturbs other people and prevents them from entering samadhi. If you can't enter samadhi, you won't be able to open up your wisdom. If you can't open up your wisdom, you won't gain a genuine awakening. So you should all help each other out on the way to enlightenment. It's important, then, that once the session starts, the talking ends.

Sutra:

> **At that time the Bodhisattva Flower Virtue said to the Buddha, "World Honored One, the Bodhisattva Wondrous Sound has deeply planted the roots of goodness. World Honored One, in what samadhi does this Bodhisattva dwell that he is able in this way to transform himself and save living beings?"**

F2. Questions and answers about the samadhi he dwells in.
G1. The question.

Commentary:

The Bodhisattva Flower Virtue wanted to know what merit and virtue Wondrous Sound Bodhisattva had cultivated to gain such great spiritual powers. Shakyamuni Buddha told him that the Bodhisattva had made offerings of a hundred thousand kinds of music to the Buddha Cloud and Thunder Sound King.

At that time the Bodhisattva Flower Virtue said to the Buddha, "World Honored One, the Bodhisattva Wondrous Sound has deeply planted the roots of goodness. Although

I know that is the case, still, **World Honored One, in what samadhi does this Bodhisattva dwell that he is able in this way to transform himself,** everywhere in all kinds of forms with as-you-will spiritual powers, **and save living beings** on such a vast scale?"

Sutra:

> **The Buddha told the Bodhisattva Flower Virtue, "Good man, this samadhi is called the Manifestation of All Physical Forms. The Bodhisattva Wondrous Sound, dwelling in this samadhi, can in this way benefit limitless living beings."**

G2. The answer.

Commentary:

The Buddha told the Bodhisattva Flower Virtue, "Good man, this samadhi is called the Manifestation of All Physical Forms. Remaining unmoving in the Way-place, he can yet manifest everywhere in the various forms of all living beings. **The Bodhisattva Wondrous Sound, dwelling in this samadhi, can in this way benefit limitless living beings."**

Sutra:

> **When this chapter on the Bodhisattva Wondrous Sound had been spoken, those who had accompanied the Bodhisattva Wondrous Sound, eighty-four thousand in all, all obtained the samadhi of the Manifestation of All Physical Forms. Limitless Bodhisattvas in the Saha world also gained this samadhi, as well as *dharani*.**

E4. Benefits gained in two lands.

Commentary:

When this chapter on the Bodhisattva Wondrous Sound had been spoken, those who had accompanied the Bodhisattva Wondrous Sound from the country Adorned with Pure Light to the Saha world, **eighty-four thousand in all, all obtained the samadhi of the Manifestation of All Physical Forms. Limitless Bodhisattvas in the Saha world also gained this samadhi as well as *dharani*,** the Dharma-door of uniting and upholding. So Bodhisattvas from both lands gained many benefits.

Sutra:

> **At that time the Bodhisattva Mahasattva Wondrous Sound, having made offerings to Shakyamuni Buddha and to the *stupa* of the Buddha Many Jewels, returned to his own country. The countries he passed through quaked in six ways, precious lotus flowers rained down, and hundreds of thousands of myriads of *kotis* of kinds of music played. When he arrived at his own country, surrounded by the eighty-four thousand Bodhisattvas, he went before the Buddha Wisdom of Pure Flower Constellation King and said, "World Honored One, I have been to the Saha world where I benefited living beings. I saw Shakyamuni Buddha and the *stupa* of Many Jewels Buddha, bowed, and made offerings to them. I also saw the Bodhisattva Manjushri, the Dharma Prince, as well as the Bodhisattva Medicine King, the Bodhisattva Who Has Gained the Power of Diligent Vigor, the Bodhisattva**

Courageous Giving, and others, and enabled eighty-four thousand Bodhisattvas to obtain the Samadhi of the Manifestation of All Physical Forms."

E5. Going back to his own country.

Commentary:

At that time the Bodhisattva Mahasattva Wondrous Sound, having made offerings to Shakyamuni Buddha and to the *stupa* of the Buddha Many Jewels of all kinds of jewels and beads, **returned to his own country**, Adorned with Pure Light. **The countries he passed through** on the way back **quaked in six ways, precious lotus flowers rained down, and hundreds of thousands of myriads of *kotis* of kinds of music played. When he arrived at his own country, surrounded by the eighty-four thousand Bodhisattvas, he went before the Buddha Wisdom of Pure Flower Constellation King and said, "World Honored One, I have been to the Saha world where I benefited living beings** extensively. **I saw Shakyamuni Buddha and the *stupa* of Many Jewels Buddha, bowed, and made offerings to them. I also saw the Bodhisattva Manjushri, the Dharma Prince,** the greatly wise Bodhisattva whose name means 'Wonderfully Auspicious,' **as well as the Bodhisattva Medicine King.** This Bodhisattva's ascetic practices are inconceivable. In past lives he burned his body and burned off his arms as an offering to the Buddha. Now, he is able to cure the sicknesses of living beings. I also saw **the Bodhisattva Who Has Gained the Power of Diligent Vigor.** He is vigorous in body and mind, and vigorous in the six periods of the day and night. He is never lazy for a second. I also encountered **the Bodhisattva Courageous**

Giving and others. This Bodhisattva is even more inconceivable. No matter what living beings seek from him, he gives it to them. He even gives away his very life, head, eyes, brain, and marrow; his countries, cities, wives, and children. He gives it all away.

"**And** I **enabled eighty-four thousand Bodhisattvas to obtain the samadhi of the Manifestation of All Physical Forms.** My trip to the Saha world really paid off for living beings. It was great."

Sutra:

> **When this chapter on the comings and goings of the Bodhisattva Wondrous Sound had been spoken, forty-two thousand gods obtained the patience with the Nonproduction of Dharmas. The Bodhisattva Flower Virtue obtained the Dharma Flower Samadhi.**

E6. Hearing the chapter and entering the Way.

Commentary:

When this chapter on the comings and goings of the Bodhisattva Wondrous Sound had been spoken, forty-two thousand gods obtained the patience with the Nonproduction of Dharmas. The Bodhisattva Flower Virtue, who asked about the Bodhisattva Wondrous Sound's samadhi, **obtained the Dharma Flower Samadhi.**

End of Chapter Twenty-four

Biographical Sketch of the Venerable Master Hsuan Hua

The Venerable Master, a native of Shuangcheng County in Jilin Province of China, was born on the sixteenth day of the third lunar month in the year of *wuwu* at the beginning of the century. He was named Yushu (or Yuxi) Bai. His father, Fuhai Bai, was hardworking and thrifty. His mother, maiden name Hu, ate only vegetarian food and recited the Buddha's name every day. When she was pregnant with the Master, she prayed to the Buddhas and Bodhisattvas. The night before his birth, in a dream she saw Amitabha Buddha emitting brilliant light. Following that the Master was born.

The Master was quiet and untalkative by nature, but he had a righteous and heroic spirit. As a child, he followed his mother's example and ate only vegetarian food and recited the Buddha's name. At the age of eleven, the sight of a dead infant made him aware of the great matter of birth and death, and he resolved to leave the home-life. At twelve, he heard of how Filial Son Wong (Great Master Chang Ren) of Shuangcheng County had practiced filial piety and attained the Way, and he vowed to follow the Filial Son's example. The Master decided to bow to his parents every morning and evening as a way of acknowledging his faults and repaying his parents' kindness. Because of his filial piety, he became known as Filial Son Bai.

At fifteen, he took refuge under the Venerable Master Chang Zhi. That year he began to attend school and mastered the Four Books, the Five Classics, the texts of various Chinese schools of thought, and the fields of medicine, divination, astrology, and physiognomy. He participated in the Virtue Society and other charitable societies. He explained the *Sixth Patriarch's Sutra*, the *Vajra Sutra*, and other Sutras to those who were illiterate, and he started a free school for the poor.

When he was nineteen, his mother passed away, and he requested Venerable Master Chang Zhi of Sanyuan (Three Conditions) Monastery to shave his head. He was given the Dharma name An Tse and style name To Lun. Dressed in the left-home robes, he built a simple hut by his mother's grave and lived there for three years in observance of filial piety. During that period, he made eighteen great vows (see page 226). He bowed to the *Flower Adornment Sutra*, engaged in worship and repentance, practiced meditation, studied the scriptures, ate only one meal a day, and did not lie down to sleep at night. His sincere efforts to purify and cultivate himself won the admiration of the villagers and evoked numerous miracles and responses from the Buddhas, Bodhisattvas, and Dharma-protecting gods and dragons. He came to be known as an extraordinary monk.

One day as he was sitting in meditation, he saw the Great Master, the Sixth Patriarch, come to his hut and tell him, "In the future you will go to the West and meet countless people. The living beings you teach and transform will be as countless as the sands of the Ganges River. That will mark the beginning of the Buddhadharma in the West." After saying that, the Sixth Patriarch vanished. The

Master completed his observance of filial piety and went to Changbai Mountain, where he dwelled in seclusion and practiced austerities at the Amitabha Cave. Later he returned to Sanyuan Monastery and became the leader of the assembly. During his years in Manchuria, the Master taught people according to their potentials. He awakened those who were confused and saved many lives. Countless dragons, snakes, foxes, ghosts, and spirits took refuge and received the precepts from him, changing their evil and cultivating goodness.

In 1946, the Master embarked on an arduous journey to Caoxi, Guangzhou, to pay homage to the Elder Master Hsu Yun, whom he esteemed as a great hero of Buddhism. Along the way he stayed at many renowned monasteries in China and received complete ordination at Mount Putuo in 1947. He reached Nanhua Monastery in 1948 and paid homage to Elder Master Hsu Yun. The Elder Master appointed him as an instructor and later as the Dean of Academic Affairs in the Nanhua Vinaya Academy. He saw that the Master was an outstanding individual and transmitted the Dharma to him, giving him the Dharma name Hsuan Hua and making him the Ninth Patriarch of the Wei Yang Sect, the forty-fifth generation since the First Patriarch Mahakashyapa.

In 1949, the Master bid farewell to the Elder Master Yun and went to Hong Kong. In propagating the Dharma there, he emphasized all five schools of Buddhism—Chan, Doctrine, Vinaya, Esoteric, and Pure Land. He renovated old temples, printed Sutras, and constructed images. Among the temples he established were Western Bliss Gardens Monastery, Cixing (Flourishing Compassion) Chan

Monastery, and the Buddhist Lecture Hall. During a period of over ten years, he created extensive Dharma-affinities with the people of Hong Kong. The Sutras he lectured on included the *Earth Store Sutra*, the *Vajra Sutra*, the *Amitabha Sutra*, the *Shurangama Sutra*, and the "Universal Door Chapter" of the *Dharma Flower Sutra*. He held such Dharma assemblies as the Great Compassion Repentance, the Medicine Master Repentance, and recitation and meditation sessions. He published the magazine *Hsin Fa (Mind Dharma)*. As a result of his zealous efforts to propagate the Dharma, Buddhism flourished in Hong Kong. During that time he also visited such countries as Thailand and Burma to study Theravada Buddhism. He hoped to establish communication between the Mahayana and the Theravada traditions and to unite the different sects of Buddhism.

In 1959, the Master saw that conditions were ripe in the West, and he instructed his disciples to establish the Sino-American Buddhist Association (later renamed the Dharma Realm Buddhist Association) in the United States. In 1961 he traveled to Australia and preached the Dharma for one year. Since the conditions were not yet ripe there, he returned to Hong Kong in 1962. Later that year, at the invitation of Buddhists in America, the Master traveled alone to the United States and raised the banner of the Proper Dharma at the Buddhist Lecture Hall in San Francisco. Living in a damp, windowless basement that resembled a grave, he called himself "The Monk in the Grave." When the Cuban Missile Crisis broke out, the Master embarked on a thirty-five-day fast to pray for an end to hostilities and for world peace. By the end of his fast, the crisis had been resolved.

During the Shurangama Study and Practice Summer Session in 1968, over thirty students from the University of Washington in Seattle went to San Francisco to study with the Master. At the end of the session, five of them requested permission to shave their heads and leave the home-life. That was the beginning of the Sangha in the history of American Buddhism. The Master devoted himself to propagating the Dharma, directing the translation of the Buddhist Canon, and developing education. He accepted many disciples, established monasteries, and set forth principles. He exhorted his disciples to work hard in order to cause the Proper Dharma to flourish eternally throughout the Dharma Realm.

The Master lectured on the Sutras and spoke the Dharma every day for several decades, explaining profound principles in a way that made them easy to understand. He also trained his left-home and lay disciples to explain the teachings. He led various delegations to disseminate the Dharma at various universities and in various countries around the world, with the aim of leading beings to turn toward goodness and to discover their innate wisdom.

To date over a hundred volumes of the Master's explanations of the scriptures have been translated into English, and some have also been translated into Spanish, Vietnamese, Japanese, and other languages. The Master's aim is to translate the Buddhist Canon into all the world's languages so that the Dharma will become popular worldwide.

The Master established Instilling Goodness Elementary School, Developing Virtue Secondary School, Dharma Realm Buddhist University, and the Sangha and Laity

Training Programs at the City of Ten Thousand Buddhas. Many of the branch monasteries of Dharma Realm Buddhist Association have classes for children as well. These educational programs are based on the eight virtues of filiality, fraternal respect, loyalty, trustworthiness, propriety, righteousness, incorruptibility, and a sense of shame. In order to encourage students to develop the virtues of kindness, compassion, joy, and charity and to educate them to become men and women of integrity who will be able to contribute to society, the boys and girls study separately and the volunteer teachers regard education as their personal responsibility.

The Master taught his disciples to meditate, recite the Buddha's name, practice repentance, study the Sutras, and observe the precepts strictly. He taught them to eat only one meal a day (at midday) and to always wear the precept sash. He taught them to dwell in harmony and to encourage each other. Under his guidance, a Sangha that practices and maintains the Proper Dharma has grown up in the West. The Master established the City of Ten Thousand Buddhas as an international spiritual community where students and truthseekers can study and work together for the cause of world peace and harmony among religions.

The Master's life was one of total selflessness. He vowed to take the suffering and hardships of all living beings upon himself, and to dedicate to them all the blessings and happiness that he himself ought to enjoy. He practiced what was difficult to practice and endured what was difficult to endure. No amount of hardship could deter him from fulfilling his lofty resolves. He composed a verse expressing his principles:

Freezing, we do not scheme.
Starving, we do not beg.
Dying of poverty, we ask for nothing.
According with conditions, we do not change.
Not changing, we accord with conditions.
We adhere firmly to our three great principles.
We renounce our lives to do the Buddha's work.
We take the responsibility to mold our own destinies.
We rectify our lives as the Sangha's work.
Encountering specific matters,
we understand the principles.
Understanding the principles, we apply
them in specific matters.
We carry on the single pulse of the Patriarchs'
mind-transmission.

Through his unwavering maintenance of the six guiding principles of not fighting, not being greedy, not seeking, not being selfish, not pursuing personal advantage, and not lying, he brought benefit to many. He dedicated himself to serving others and taught them with wisdom and compassion. His personal example influenced countless people to change their faults and to walk upon the pure, bright path to enlightenment.

Although the Master manifested entry into Nirvana on June 7, 1995 (the tenth day of the fifth lunar month), he constantly turns the infinite Dharma wheel. He came from empty space and returned to empty space without leaving a trace. The least we can do in return for the Master's deep and profound kindness is to carefully follow his teachings, hold to our principles, and advance vigorously toward Bodhi.

The Eighteen Great Vows of the Venerable Master Hua

1. I vow that as long as there is a single Bodhisattva in the three periods of time throughout the ten directions of the Dharma Realm, to the very end of empty space, who has not accomplished Buddhahood, I too will not attain the right enlightenment.

2. I vow that as long as there is a single Pratyekabuddha in the three periods of time throughout the ten directions of the Dharma Realm, to the very end of empty space, who has not accomplished Buddhahood, I too will not attain the right enlightenment.

3. I vow that as long as there is a single Shravaka in the three periods of time throughout the ten directions of the Dharma Realm, to the very end of empty space, who has not accomplished Buddhahood, I too will not attain the right enlightenment.

4. I vow that as long as there is a single god in the Triple Realm who has not accomplished Buddhahood, I too will not attain the right enlightenment.

5. I vow that as long as there is a single human being in the worlds of the ten directions who has not accomplished Buddhahood, I too will not attain the right enlightenment.

6. I vow that as long as there is a single asura who has not accomplished Buddhahood, I too will not attain the right enlightenment.

7. I vow that as long as there is a single animal who has not accomplished Buddhahood, I too will not attain the right enlightenment.

8. I vow that as long as there is a single hungry ghost who has not accomplished Buddhahood, I too will not attain the right enlightenment.

9. I vow that as long as there is a single hell-dweller who has not accomplished Buddhahood, I too will not attain the right enlightenment.

10. I vow that as long as there is a single god, immortal, human, *asura*, air-bound or water-bound creature, animate or inanimate object, or a single dragon, beast, ghost, or spirit, and so forth, of the spiritual realm that has taken refuge with me and has not accomplished Buddhahood, I too will not attain the right enlightenment.

11. I vow to fully dedicate all blessings and happiness which I myself ought to receive and enjoy to all living beings of the Dharma Realm.

12. I vow to fully take upon myself all sufferings and hardships of all the living beings in the Dharma Realm.

13. I vow to manifest innumerable bodies as a means to gain access into the minds of living beings throughout the universe who do not believe in the Buddhadharma,

causing them to correct their faults and tend toward wholesomeness, repent of their errors and start anew, take refuge in the Triple Jewel, and ultimately accomplish Buddhahood.

14. I vow that all living beings who see my face or even hear my name will fix their thoughts on Bodhi and quickly accomplish the Buddha Way.

15. I vow to respectfully observe the Buddha's instructions and cultivate the practice of eating only one meal per day.

16. I vow to enlighten all sentient beings, universally responding to the multitude of differing potentials.

17. I vow to obtain the five eyes, six spiritual powers, and the freedom of being able to fly in this very life.

18. I vow that all of my vows will certainly be fulfilled.

Conclusion:

I vow to save the innumerable living beings.
I vow to eradicate the inexhaustible afflictions.
I vow to study the illimitable Dharma-doors.
I vow to accomplish the unsurpassed Buddha Way.

Glossary

Amitabha Buddha The Buddha of the Western Land of Ultimate Bliss. He is known as Amitabha, "infinite light," and as Amitayus, "infinite life."

Anagamin See Arhat.

Ananda Shakyamuni Buddha's cousin who served as his attendant after leaving home. After the Buddha's Nirvana, Ananda directed the compiling of the Buddhist canon. His name means "rejoicing," and among the Buddha's disciples he was foremost in erudition.

anuttarasamyaksambodhi Sanskrit for "unsurpassed, proper and equal, right enlightenment." This is the enlightenment attained by Buddhas.

Arhat Also see Two Vehicles and Hearers. There are four stages of Arhatship.

1) The Arhat of the first stage is called a 'stream-enterer' (Srotaapanna). He has entered the stream of the Dharma-nature of the sage, and he goes counter to the flow of the stream of the six senses of common people. He still has to undergo seven more rebirths in the heavens and among humans before he comes to the end of the Path.
2) The Arhat of the second stage is called a 'once-returner' (Sakridagamin). He has one more birth to undergo in the heavens and one among humans.
3) The Arhat of the third stage is called a 'never-returner' (Anagamin). He does not have to undergo birth again in the human realm.

4) The Arhat of the fourth stage is called 'unborn.' The fourth stage Arhat has attained patience with the non-production of dharmas.

asuras See eightfold division.

Avici Hell Avici is Sanskrit for "unintermittent." There are five ways in which the sufferings in this hell are unintermittent.

Bhikshu A fully-ordained Buddhist monk, one who leads a pure and celibate life and upholds 250 precepts.

Bhikshuni A fully-ordained Buddhist nun, one who leads a pure and celibate life and upholds 348 precepts.

Bodhi resolve (In Sanskrit, *bodhicitta*.) The resolve to achieve Bodhi (enlightenment) through spiritual practice.

Bodhisattva An enlightened being who does not enter Nirvana but chooses instead to remain in the world and save living beings.

Bodhisattva Way (Path) Refers to the path of spiritual practice whereby one enlightens both oneself and others, saves both oneself and others.

Brahma Heavens Refers to the Four Dhyana Heavens (see gods).

Buddha One who has achieved the ultimate, perfect enlightenment.

Buddha Recitation Session A period of time (usually a week) devoted exclusively to recitation of the Buddha's name.

Buddhadharma The methods of cultivation taught by the Buddha that lead beings to enlightenment.

Chan Session A period of time devoted entirely to meditation.

chandana A kind of sandalwood used for incense.

cultivation The practical application of the methods taught by the Buddha that lead to enlightenment.

demons From the Sanskrit *mara*, the term means "bringer of death."

dharani A *dharani*, sometimes called "mantra," unites all dharmas (phenomena) and holds infinite meanings. "Dharani" also means absolute control over good and evil influences.

dharma 1) A generic term for all the various kinds of things or entities that exist in the world, including both physical and mental phenomena. 2) A method.

Dharma (Also: Buddhadharma.) The teachings of the Buddha.

Dharma-door A method of practice.

Dharma-Ending Age The last of the three ages of Dharma. After the Buddha speaks the Dharma, there follows the Proper Dharma Age, which lasts 1000 years. It is followed by the Dharma Image Age, which also lasts 1000 years. The last period is the Dharma-Ending Age, the age strong in fighting, which lasts for 10,000 years. During this age, the understanding and practice of the Buddha's teachings gradually decline and finally disappear.

Dharma Master A teacher of Dharma. A respectful term of address for members of the Sangha.

Dharma-wheel Turning the Dharma-wheel refers to explaining and propagating the teachings of Buddhism, and also to the physical embodying and functioning of these teachings in practice.

dhyana A Sanskrit word which translates as "stilling one's thoughts" and refers to meditation. *Chan* in Chinese, *zen* in Japanese.

division-bodies These could be said to be "divisions of the spirit," "divisions of the nature," and "divisions of the heart" (of the Buddha). They may also be called "transformation bodies," which are likened to the reflection of the one moon in many waters. The substance of the moon does not change, no matter how many reflections appear.

eight difficulties Eight conditions in which it is difficult to study the Buddhadharma, namely
1) being born in the hells;
2) being born as a hungry ghost;
3) being born as an animal;

4) being born in the northern continent of Uttarakuru;
5) being born in the Long-life Heaven;
6) being born at a time before or after a Buddha is in the world;
7) being born with impaired faculties (blind, deaf, mute, etc.);
8) being endowed with worldly intelligence or clever argumentative skill.

eightfold division Eight classes of spiritual beings who act as protectors of the Buddhas' teachings. They are: gods; dragons; *yakshas*, "speedy ghosts"; *gandharvas*, "musical spirits"; *asuras*, "beings that like to fight"; *garudas*, "golden-winged peng birds"; *kinnaras*, another kind of "musical spirits"; and *mahoragas*, "great pythons."

Enlightened to Conditions (Pratyekabuddha) One who attains enlightenment through contemplating the Twelve Causes and Conditions.

Equal Enlightenment The level of enlightenment of Bodhisattvas immediately preceding Buddhahood.

externalists Adherents of heterodox religions, cults, and sects that seek for enlightenment externally, outside the mind.

four assemblies The assemblies of Bhikshus, Bhikshunis, Upasakas, and Upasikas

Five Precepts The fundamental precepts received by laity, they are: no killing, no stealing, no sexual misconduct, no lying, and no intoxicants (including cigarettes and drugs of all kinds).

flesh cowl The flesh protuberance on top of the Buddha's head. It is one of the thirty-two hallmarks of the Buddhas.

gandharvas See eightfold division.

Ganges River A 1550-mile-long river in northern India, originating in the Himalayas and flowing east to the Bay of Bengal. Its sands are said to be as fine as flour. Thus, in Buddhist scriptures, the expression "Ganges' sands" is used as an analogy for an unreckonable number.

garudas See eightfold division.

gods Gods, according to Buddhist teaching, live in various heavens. They are not immortal or omnipotent. They do have long lifespans and various spiritual powers. Any one can be reborn as a god by generating the appropriate good karma; however, gods are not enlightened. They eventually die and are reborn in lower realms according to their karma.

The heavens in which the gods reside are divided into three basic categories: 1) the Six Desire Heavens, 2) the Four Dhyana Heavens, and 3) the Four Formless Realms.

good roots Good roots are the firm foundation which comes from cultivation. A good foundation causes your Dharma-body to manifest and your inherent wisdom to function. It is essential to plant good roots before the Triple Jewel in order to reap the fruit of Bodhi.

Great Strength Bodhisattva (In Sanskrit, Mahasthamaprapta Bodhisattva.) The Bodhisattva who, along with Guanyin Bodhisattva, dwells with Amitabha Buddha in the Western Pure Land and helps that Buddha to teach living beings. Mindfulness of the Buddha is the method by which he achieved sagehood.

Great Vehicle This is a translation of the Sanskrit term *Mahayana* and refers to the vehicle of the Bodhisattvas that is large enough to hold and carry across all living beings. In these compassionate teachings the Buddha stressed enlightening both oneself and others, saving both oneself and others.

Guanshiyin Bodhisattva (In Sanskrit, Avalokiteshvara Bodhisattva.) Of the four great Bodhisattvas who have affinities with our world, Guanshiyin or Guanyin is the Bodhisattva of Great Compassion. His name means "Contemplating the World's Sounds."

Guanyin Session A session, usually one week long, for intensive practice of reciting Guanyin Bodhisattva's name.

Hearers *Shravakas* in Sanskrit, also known as *Arhats,* these are the Buddha's disciples who awaken to the Way by hearing the sound of the Buddha's teachings.

Heaven of the Thirty-three Known as Trayastrimsha in Sanskrit, this heaven is one of the Six Desire Heavens (see gods) and corresponds to the Christian heaven.

kalpa A Sanskrit word which means "a long span of time," an eon.

1 *kalpa*	=139,000 years
1,000 *kalpas*	=1 small *kalpa*
20 small *kalpas*	=1 middle-sized *kalpa*
4 middle-sized *kalpas*	=1 great *kalpa*

kinnaras See eightfold division.

koti One of a series of very large numbers used in ancient India.

Jambudvipa One of the four great continents in a world. This is the southern continent, the one we live in.

left-home people A generic term for Buddhist monks and nuns.

mahoragas See eightfold division.

Manjushri Bodhisattva Of the four great Bodhisattvas who have affinities with our world, Manjushri Bodhisattva is the Bodhisattva of Great Wisdom. His name is explained as meaning "Wonderful Virtue" or "Wonderfully Auspicious."

Middle Way The Buddhist concept of moderation, which advocates avoiding extremes by balancing oneself in the midst of dualities.

Mount Sumeru The Sanskrit word Sumeru means "Wonderfully High." It is the central mountain of every world.

Namo A Sanskrit word that means "homage to" or "return one's life to."

nayuta One of a series of very large numbers used in ancient India.

Nirvana Nirvana is a Sanskrit term that is interpreted in various ways: (1) cessation, or extinction, referring to the elimination of afflictions at the time of enlightenment or to the ceasing to be of the *skandhas* when an enlightened person at death chooses to be reborn no longer; (2) freedom from desire; and (3) no longer either coming into being or ceasing to be.

One Vehicle The One Buddha Vehicle, that is, the ultimate Vehicle (teaching) for achieving Buddhahood, which is revealed by the Buddha in the *Dharma Flower Sutra* at the end of his teaching career.

prajna Transcendental wisdom.

precepts Rules of ethical conduct set forth by the Buddha to help cultivators regulate their bodies, mouths, and minds. In Buddhism, there are 5 precepts for laypeople, 10 precepts for novices, 250 precepts for fully ordained monks and 348 precepts for fully-ordained nuns, and 10 major and 48 minor Bodhisattva precepts for those who bring forth the Bodhisattva resolve.

Pratyekabuddha See Enlightened to Conditions.

precepts Rules for moral and ethical conduct.

Saha The name of the world we live in, meaning "able to endure." This refers to how beings in this world are able to bear its sufferings and even consider them to be bliss.

Sakridagamin See Arhat.

samadhi Concentration attained through meditation and other practices. There are many types and levels of *samadhi*.

Ten Good Deeds Opposite of the Ten Evils, they are three of the body: no killing, no stealing, no sexual misconduct; three of the mind: no greed, no hatred, no stupidity; and four of the mouth: no harsh speech, no backbiting, no lying, and no loose speech.

Sangha The order of Buddhist monks and nuns.

Sanskrit An ancient Indian language belonging to the Indic branch of the Indo-European family of languages; the language that the Mahayana Buddhist Sutras were preserved in.

seven treasures Gold, silver, lapis lazuli, crystal, mother-of-pearl, red pearls, and carnelian.

Shakyamuni Buddha *Shakyamuni* is a Sanskrit word. *Shakya*, the Buddha's family name, means "able to be humane." *Muni* is the Buddha's personal name and means "still and silent." The most recent Buddha to appear in our world, he realized enlightenment and then taught in India around three thousand years ago. Actually, Shakyamuni Buddha first realized Buddhahood many, many lifetimes ago.

sharira A Sanskrit word that means "efficacious bones"; these are jewel-like relics that remain after cremation of an accomplished cultivator.

Shurangama Sutra One of the most important Mahayana Sutras in Buddhism, it will be the first Sutra to disappear in the Dharma-Ending Age.

six perfections The practices of Bodhisattvas, also called the six *paramitas*, they are: giving, holding precepts, patience, vigor, samadhi, and wisdom.

six realms of rebirth (Also: six paths.) The destinies where common, unenlightened beings revolve within the cycle of birth and death. These realms are those of gods, *asuras*, humans, animals, hungry ghosts, and hell-beings.

Small Vehicle The Buddha's teaching to Hearers and Pratyekabuddhas, which emphasizes enlightening and liberating oneself, but not others.

spiritual penetrations There are six spiritual powers or penetrations: 1) the heavenly eye, 2) the heavenly ear, 3) knowledge of others' thoughts, 4) knowledge of past lives, 5) complete spirit, and 6) having no outflows. These abilities come naturally as a part of cultivation, but are not the goal of cultivation.

Srotaapanna See Arhat.

stupa A pagoda built in memory of enlighened sages and masters, and perhaps housing their crematory relics or flesh body.

Subhuti The Buddha's disciple who was foremost in understanding emptiness.

three thousand great thousand worlds One thousand worlds make up one small thousand world system. A thousand of these make up one middle thousand world system. A thousand of these make up one great thousand world system. Because a thousand is multiplied three times, these one billion (1,000,000,000) worlds are also called the "three thousand great thousand worlds".

Sutras Discourses spoken by Buddhas, Bodhisattvas, or other qualified sages.

ten directions North, south, east, west, northeast, northwest, southeast, southwest, above, and below.

thirty-two marks Hallmarks of all Buddhas, extending from the crowns of their heads to the soles of their feet, achieved through the perfection of blessings and wisdom.

Thus Come One (In Sanskrit, Tathagata.) One of the ten titles of a Buddha.

Tiantai School One of the two major Chinese schools of classification of the Buddha's teachings.

Triple Jewel The Buddha, the Dharma, and the Sangha.

Twelve Causes and Conditions Those Enlightened to Conditions (Pratyekabuddhas) become enlightened by contemplating both the arising and the cessation of these twelve, which condition each other in the following sequence:

1. ignorance is the condition for activity;
2. activity is the condition for consciousness;
3. consciousness is the condition for name and form;
4. name and form are the condition for the six sense faculties;
5. the six sense faculties are the condition for contact;
6. contact is the condition for feeling;
7. feeling is the condition for emotional love;
8. emotional love is the condition for grasping;
9. grasping is the condition for becoming;
10. becoming is the condition for birth;

11. birth is the condition for
12. old age and death.

Two Vehicles The vehicles of Hearers and Those Enlightened to Conditions. From the point of view of the Great Vehicle, these are considered to be lesser vehicles.

Upasaka, Upasika Sanskrit terms for a Buddhist layman and a Buddhist laywoman, respectively.

vaidurya One of the seven treasures, this translucent blue-green gem is sometimes translated as lapis lazuli or crystal.

vajra A Sanskrit word meaning "durable," "luminous," and "able to cut." It is indestructible and usually represented by diamond.

Way-place (In Sanskrit, Bodhimanda.) Any place of practice—a temple, a monastery, a hermitage—regardless of its size.

Western Land of Ultimate Bliss (In Sanskrit, Sukhavati.) Amitabha Buddha's pure land. By the power of his vows, Amitabha Buddha leads all beings to rebirth in his country, where they realize Buddhahood. This power attracts living beings to the Western Land of Ultimate Bliss, just as a magnet attracts iron filings. If living beings do not attain enlightenment, Amitabha Buddha himself won't realize Buddhahood either.

World Honored One (In Sanskrit, Bhagavan.) One of the ten titles held in common by all Buddhas. Buddhas are honored by those in the world and those beyond the world.

yakshas See eightfold division.

yojana An Indian measure of distance, one small *yojana* equals about 13 English miles; a middle-sized *yojana* is about 20 English miles; and a big *yojana* is about 27 English miles.

Index

E

F

G

H

J

K

L

M

N

O

P

Q

S

T

V

Verse of Transference

May the merit and virtue accrued from this work,
Adorn the Buddhas' Pure Lands,
Repaying four kinds of kindness above,
And aiding those suffering in the paths below.
May those who see and hear of this,
All bring forth the resolve for Bodhi,
And when this retribution body is over,
Be born together in the Land of Ultimate Bliss.

Namo Dharma Protector
Wei Tuo Bodhisattva

Buddhist Text Translation Society Publications

Buddhist Text Translation Society
International Translation Institute
1777 Murchison Drive
Burlingame, California 94010-4504 USA
Phone: 650-692-5912 Fax: 650-692-5056

When Buddhism first came to China from India, one of the most important tasks required for its establishment was the translation of the Buddhist scriptures from Sanskrit into Chinese. This work involved a great many people, such as the renowned monk National Master Kumarajiva (fifth century), who led an assembly of over 800 people to work on the translation of the Tripitaka (Buddhist canon) for over a decade. Because of the work of individuals such as these, nearly the entire Buddhist Tripitaka of over a thousand texts exists to the present day in Chinese.

Now the banner of the Buddha's Teachings is being firmly planted in Western soil, and the same translation work is being done from Chinese into English. Since 1970, the Buddhist Text Translation Society (BTTS) has been making a paramount contribution toward this goal. Aware that the Buddhist Tripitaka is a work of such magnitude that its translation could never be entrusted to a single person, the BTTS, emulating the translation assemblies of ancient times, does not publish a work until it has passed through four committees for primary translation, revision, editing, and certification. The leaders of these committees are

Bhikshus (monks) and Bhikshunis (nuns) who have devoted their lives to the study and practice of the Buddha's teachings. For this reason, all of the works of the BTTS put an emphasis on what the principles of the Buddha's teachings mean in terms of actual practice and not simply hypothetical conjecture.

The translations of canonical works by the Buddhist Text Translation Society are accompanied by extensive commentaries by the Venerable Tripitaka Master Hsuan Hua and are available in softcover only unless otherwise noted.

Buddhist Sutras

Amitabha Sutra. This Sutra, which was spoken by the Buddha without having been formally requested as other Sutras were, explains the causes and circumstances for rebirth in the Land of Ultimate Bliss of Amitabha (Limitless Light) Buddha. The commentary includes extensive information on common Buddhist terminology and stories about many of the Buddha's foremost disciples. ISBN 0-917512-01-4. 204 pp. $8.00.

(**Explicación General del Sutra en que El Buda Habla de Amitabha.** Spanish edition. ISBN 0-917512-30-6. $8.00.)

Dharma Flower (Lotus) Sutra. In this Sutra, which was spoken in the last period of the Buddha's teaching, the Buddha proclaims the ultimate principles of the Dharma, which unite all previous teachings into one. When completed, the translation of the entire Sutra and commentary will comprise an estimated fifteen to twenty volumes. The following are those volumes that have been published to date. Set of ten volumes, $79.50.

Volume I. Foreword by Venerable Master Hua. Discusses the five periods and the eight teachings of the T'ien T'ai School and then analyzes the School's Five Profound Meanings as they relate to the Sutra. The last portion tells of the life of Tripitaka Master Kumarajiva, who translated the Sutra from Sanskrit into Chinese. ISBN 0-917512-16-2. 85 pp.

Volume II. Chapter One, Introduction. Describes the setting for the speaking of the Sutra, the assembly that gathered to hear it, the Buddha's emission of light, the questions asked by Maitreya Bodhisattva, and the response given by Manjushri Bodhisattva. ISBN 0-917512-22-7. 324 pp.

Volume III. Chapter Two, Expedient Methods. After the Buddha emerges from samadhi, he speaks of the vast merit and virtue of the Buddhas. Shariputra beseeches him to expound further on this. After his third request, the Buddha consents and for the first time proclaims that all beings without exception can become Buddhas.
ISBN 0-917512-26-X. 183 pp.

Volume IV. Chapter Three, A Parable. The Buddha explains the purpose of his teachings by means of an analogy of an elder who tries to rescue five hundred children who are absorbed in play in a burning house. ISBN 0-917512-62-6. 371 pp.

Volume V. Chapter Four, Belief and Understanding. Four of the Buddha's foremost Arhat disciples relate a parable about a prodigal son to express their joy upon hearing that they, too, can become Buddhas in the future.
ISBN 0-917512-64-2. 200 pp.

Volume VI. Chapter Five, Medicinal Herbs and **Chapter Six, Conferring Predictions.** The Buddha uses the analogy of a rain cloud to illustrate how his teaching benefits all beings with total impartiality. He also predicts that the previously mentioned Arhat disciples will become Buddhas in the future. In bestowing his prediction, he tells what their future Buddha names will be and what the names of their world systems and *kalpas* will be, as well as the scope of their Dharma.
ISBN 0-917512-65-0. 161 pp.

Volume VII. Chapter Seven, Parable of the Transformation City. The Buddha teaches that the attainment of his Arhat disciples is like a city that he conjured up as an expedient when they became weary of the journey to Buddhahood.
ISBN 0-917512-67-7. 250 pp.

Volume VIII. Chapter Eight, Five Hundred Disciples Receive Predictions and **Chapter Nine, Bestowing Predictions upon**

Those Studying and Beyond Study. More than a thousand disciples receive predictions that they will become Buddhas in the future. ISBN 0-917512-71-5. 160 pp.

Volume IX. Chapter Ten, Masters of the Dharma and **Chapter Eleven, Vision of the Jewelled Stupa.** Chapter Ten explains the vast merit from upholding and propagating the *Wonderful Dharma Lotus Flower Sutra*. In Chapter Eleven, all of the many millions of transformation bodies of Shakyamuni Buddha gather in one place so that those in the assembly can see Many Jewels Buddha, who in the distant past made a vow to appear wherever this Sutra is spoken. ISBN 0-917512-85-5. 270 pp.

Volume X. Chapter Twelve, Devadatta and **Chapter Thirteen, Exhortation to Maintain.** In Chapter Twelve, the Buddha reveals that Devadatta was once his teacher in a former life, and then bestows a prediction of Buddhahood on him. The eight-year-old dragon girl becomes a Buddha. In Chapter Thirteen, the Buddha bestows predictions of Buddhahood on Bhikshunis. ISBN 0-917512-52-9. 150 pp.

Flower Adornment (Avatamsaka) Sutra. Known as the "King of Kings" of all Buddhist scriptures because of its profundity and great length (81 rolls containing more than 700,000 Chinese characters), this Sutra contains the most complete explanation of the Buddha's state and the Bodhisattva's quest for Awakening. When completed, the entire Sutra text with commentary will comprise from 75 to 100 volumes. The following are those volumes that have been published to date:

Verse Preface. A succinct and eloquent verse commentary by T'ang Dynasty National Master Ch'ing Liang, the Master of seven emperors. The Preface gives a complete explanation of all the fundamental principles contained in the Sutra. This is the first English translation of this text. Bilingual edition, English/Chinese. ISBN 0-917512-28-6. 244 pp. $7.00.

Prologue. A detailed explanation of the principles of the Sutra, by National Master Ch'ing Liang, utilizing the Hsien Shou method of analyzing scriptures known as the Ten Doors. The *Prologue* contains the first Nine Doors. Will be approximately seven to ten volumes upon completion. Set of four books, $38.00. The following volumes have been published to date:

First Door. The Causes and Conditions for the Arising of the Teaching of the *Flower Adornment Sutra*. Complete in one volume. ISBN 0-917512-66-9. 252 pp.

Second Door. The Stores and Teachings in Which It Is Contained. Three volumes as follows:

Part One. Complete discussion of the Three Stores. Beginning of discussion of the Schools in China. ISBN 0-917512-73-1. 280 pp.

Part Two. More on Chinese schools. The Indian schools and comparisons between them. ISBN 0-917512-98-7. 220 pp.

Part Three. Detailed discussion of the Five Hsien Shou Teachings, the sequence of the Teaching Methods, and the inconceivable state of the Flower Adornment. Completes the explanation of the Second Door. ISBN 0-88139-009-7. 160 pp.

The following twenty-two volumes are available as a set only. $174.50.

Flower Store Adorned Sea of Worlds, Chapter Five, Parts One & Two. Describes the universe we live in, including an explanation of principles pertaining to the coming into being of worlds, the wind wheels that uphold them, their orbits, and their mutual attraction. Also, detailed descriptions of the worlds located on the twenty tiers of the lotus that forms the basis of our cosmic structure. ISBN 0-917512-54-5. 250 pp.

Flower Store Adorned Sea of Worlds, Chapter Five, Part Three, and **Vairochana, Chapter Six.** Conclusion of Chapter Five, "Flower Store Adorned Sea of Worlds," and Chapter Six, "Vairochana," which discusses the causes and conditions of the clear, pure Dharma-body Buddha, Vairochana Buddha. ISBN 0-88139-114-X. 191 pp.

The Names of the Thus Come Ones, Chapter Seven, and **The Four Holy Truths, Chapter Eight.** In Chapter Seven, the Bodhisattvas gather from the worlds of the ten directions to request that the Buddha speak about the Great Bodhisattva practices, which are explained at great length in later chapters of the *Flower Adornment Sutra.* In Chapter Eight, each of the Four Holy Truths—suffering, accumulation, extinction, and the Way—are explained according to the conditions of ten different worlds plus the Saha World, the world that we inhabit. ISBN 0-88139-014-3. 77 pp.

Bright Enlightenment, Chapter Nine. From the soles of his feet, Shakyamuni Buddha emits light, which continually gets brighter and shines upon more and more different countries in the ten directions. After each time that he emits light, Manjushri Bodhisattva speaks verses praising the virtues of the Buddha. ISBN 0-88139-005-4. 225 pp.

Pure Conduct, Chapter Eleven. This chapter of the Sutra gives a detailed explanation of the pure practices of the Bodhisattva. It is one of the most renowned guides to the Vinaya in the Buddhist canon. ISBN 0-917512-37-5. 255 pp.

Ten Dwellings, Chapter Fifteen. Explains the state of the Ten Dwellings attained by the Bodhisattva.
ISBN 0-917512-77-4. 185 pp.

Brahma Conduct, Chapter Sixteen. Explains the meanings of the pure Brahma conduct cultivated by the Bodhisattva. ISBN 0-917512-80-4. 65 pp.

The Merit and Virtue from First Bringing forth the Mind, Chapter Seventeen. Various analogies describe the merit obtained by the Bodhisattva when he first resolves his mind on becoming enlightened. ISBN 0-917512-83-9. 200 pp.

The Ten Inexhaustible Treasuries, Chapter Twenty-two. Explains the Ten Inexhaustible Treasuries attained by the Bodhisattva immediately following the Ten Conducts. ISBN 0-917512-38-3. 184 pp.

Praises in the Tushita Heaven, Chapter Twenty-four. Verses in praise of the Buddha spoken by the great Bodhisattvas after the Buddha arrived in the Tushita Heaven, prior to Vajra Banner Bodhisattva's explanation of the Ten Transferences. ISBN 0-917512-39-1. 130 pp.

Ten Grounds, Chapter Twenty-six, Part One. Contains the First Ground of Happiness, which focuses on the practice of giving. ISBN 0-917512-87-1. 234 pp.

Part Two. Covers the Bodhisattva's Second Ground of Leaving Filth, Third Ground of Emitting Light, and Fourth Ground of Blazing Wisdom. ISBN 0-917512-74-X. 200 pp.

Universal Worthy's Conduct, Chapter Thirty-six. Universal Worthy Bodhisattva explains obstructions that arise from anger; gives methods to correct it when it does arise; and describes the purities, wisdoms, universal entrances, and supremely wondrous minds that result. ISBN 0-88139-011-9. 75 pp.

Entering the Dharma Realm, Chapter Thirty-nine. This chapter, which makes up one quarter of the entire Sutra, contains the spiritual journey of the Youth Good Wealth in his search for Ultimate Awakening. During his quest, he meets fifty-three Good Teachers, each of whom represents a successive stage on the Bodhisattva path. This is the first English translation of this chapter.

Part One. Describes the setting for the Youth's quest and his meeting with Manjushri Bodhisattva. ISBN 0-917512-68-5. 280 pp.

Part Two. In this volume Good Wealth meets his first ten teachers, who represent the positions of the Ten Dwellings. ISBN 0-917512-70-7. 250 pp.

Part Three. In this volume Good Wealth is taught by the ten teachers who correspond to the Ten Conducts. ISBN 0-917512-72-3. 250 pp.

Part Four. In this volume Good Wealth meets the ten teachers who represent the Bodhisattvas of the Ten Transferences. ISBN 0-917512-76-6. 185 pp.

Part Five. In this volume Good Wealth meets the six teachers who represent the first six Grounds. ISBN 0-917512-81-2. 300 pp.

Part Six. Good Wealth meets the teachers on the seventh to tenth Grounds. ISBN 0-917512-48-0. 320 pp.

Part Seven. Uniting with Conditions and Entering the True Mark. Good Wealth visits eleven teachers. ISBN 0-88139-050-X. 156 pp.

Part Eight. The Youth Good Wealth visits his final three teachers, the Bodhisattvas Maitreya, Manjushri, and Universal Worthy. ISBN 0-88139-055-0. 224 pp.

Universal Worthy's Conduct and Vows, Chapter Forty. A detailed explanation of Universal Worthy Bodhisattva's ten great kinds of practice, considered to be the foremost of all practices. ISBN 0-917512-84-7. 300 pp.

Heart Sutra & Verses without a Stand. Considered the most popular Sutra in the world today, the text of the *Heart Sutra* explains the meaning of Prajna-paramita, the perfection of wisdom that is able to clearly perceive the emptiness of all phenomena. Each line in the text is accompanied by an eloquent verse by the Venerable Master Hsuan Hua and his commentary, which contains an explanation of most of the fundamental Buddhist concepts. ISBN 0-917512-27-8. 160 pp. $7.50.

Shurangama Sutra. This Sutra gives the most detailed explanation of the Buddha's teachings concerning the mind. It includes an analysis of where the mind is located, an explanation of the origin of the cosmos, a discussion of the specific workings of *karma,* a description of all the realms of existence, and an exposition on the fifty kinds of deviant samadhi-concentrations, which can delude us in our search for awakening. Also, in this Sutra twenty-five enlightened sages explain the methods they used to become enlightened. Set of first seven volumes $59.50.

Volume One. The Venerable Ananda presents seven ideas on the location of the mind. The Buddha shows how each one is incorrect and then explains the roots of the false and the true. ISBN 0-917512-17-0. 289 pp.

Volume Two. The Buddha explains individual and collective karma, and he reveals the true mind by displaying ten different aspects of the seeing nature.
ISBN 0-917512-25-1. 212 pp.

Volume Three. The Buddha gives a clear description of the qualities of all the sense fields, their respective consciousnesses, and all the internal and external elemental forces of the universe. He explains how all are ultimately unreal, neither existing through causes nor arising spontaneously.
ISBN 0-917512-94-4. 240 pp.

Volume Four. The Buddha talks about the formation of the world, the coming into being of sentient creatures, and the cycle of karmic retribution. ISBN 0-917512-95-2. 200 pp.

Volume Five. Twenty-five sages explain the method each used to transcend the realm of birth and death. Manjushri Bodhisattva selects the method used by the Bodhisattva Kuan Yin of "returning the hearing to listen to the self-nature" as the most appropriate for people in our world system. ISBN 0-917512-96-0. 250 pp.

Volume Six. Includes the Buddha's explanation of the Four Clear and Unalterable Instructions on Purity, how to establish a Bodhimanda, the Shurangama Mantra and its wondrous functions, and the twelve categories of living beings. ISBN 0-917512-97-9. 200 pp.

Volume Seven. Contains an explanation of the fifty-five stages of the Bodhisattva's path to Enlightenment and of how beings fall into the hells and turn in the realms of the ghosts, animals, people, immortals, *asuras,* and the various heavens. ISBN 0-917512-93-6. 270 pp.

Volume Eight. This final volume presents an exposition on fifty deviant mental states associated with the five *skandhas*. In addition to being an invaluable guide for Buddhist practitioners, it offers a framework for the classification of all spiritual experience, both Buddhist and non-Buddhist.
English only, hardcover, ISBN 0-88139-401-7. 453 pp. $20.00.
Bilingual, hardcover, ISBN 0-88139-400-9. 697 pp. $25.00.

Sixth Patriarch Sutra. One of the foremost scriptures of Ch'an Buddhism, this text describes the life and teachings of the remarkable Patriarch of the T'ang Dynasty, Great Master Hui Neng, who, though unable to read or write, was enlightened to the true nature of all things.

Softcover, ISBN 0-917512-19-7. 317 pp. $10.00.
Hardcover, ISBN 0-917512-33-2. 317 pp. $15.00.

Sutra in Forty-two Sections. In this Sutra, which was the first to be transported from India and translated into Chinese, the Buddha gives the most essential instructions for cultivating the Dharma, emphasizing the cardinal virtues of renunciation, contentment, and patience.

First edition, ISBN 0-917512-15-4. 114 pp. $5.00.

Second edition, hardcover, bilingual, ISBN 0-88139-184-0. 347 pp. $12.00.

Sutra of the Past Vows of Earth Store Bodhisattva. This Sutra tells how Earth Store Bodhisattva attained his position among the greatest Bodhisattvas as the Foremost in Vows. It also explains the workings of *karma,* how beings undergo rebirth, and the various kinds of hells. This is the first English translation. Hardcover only, ISBN 0-917512-09-X. 235 pp. $16.00.
English text, without commentary, for recitation also available: ISBN 0-88139-502-1. 120 pp. $7.00

Vajra Prajna Paramita (Diamond) Sutra. One of the most popular scriptures, the *Vajra Sutra* explains how the Bodhisattva relies on the perfection of wisdom to teach and transform beings. ISBN 0-917512-02-2. 192 pp. $8.00.

Commentarial Literature

Buddha Root Farm. A collection of lectures given during an Amitabha Buddha recitation session, explaining the practice and philosophy of the Pure Land School. The instructions are very thorough and especially useful for the beginner.
ISBN 0-917512-11-1. 72 pp. $4.00.

City of 10,000 Buddhas Recitation Handbook. Contains all the material covered in the traditional morning, afternoon, and evening services and special services recited daily in Buddhist monasteries in the East and West. Includes scriptures, praises, chants, mantras, repentances, and so forth. Bilingual edition. Chinese/English. ISBN 0-88139-167-0. 240 pp. $7.00.

Filiality: The Human Source. Filiality is the very root of Way virtue. It is the single most vital force that sustains the universe. Therefore, it is only natural that Buddhist disciples base their conduct on an attitude of filial piety and respect for their parents and elders; for the rulers and officials of countries and the world; for the Triple Jewel; and ultimately for all living beings. All beings have at one time or another been our parents. Volumes I and II of this series contain stories from the twenty-four famous tales of filial paragons of China and numerous excerpts from Buddhist Sutras about filial behavior.
Volume One, ISBN 0-88139-006-2, 120 pp. $7.00.
Volume Two, ISBN 0-88139-020-8. 120 pp. $7.00.

Herein Lies the Treasure-trove. Various talks given by the Venerable Master at the City of 10,000 Buddhas.
Volume One, ISBN 0-88139-001-1. 250 pp. $6.50.
Volume Two, ISBN 0-88139-115-8. 150 pp. $6.50.

Listen to Yourself, Think Everything Over. Instructions on how to practice the method of reciting the names of the Buddhas and Bodhisattvas. Also includes a straightforward explanation of how to cultivate Ch'an meditation. All instructions were given during actual meditation and recitation sessions.
Volume One, ISBN 0-917512-24-3. 153 pp. $7.00.
Volume Two, ISBN 0-88139-010-0. 200 pp. $7.00.

Shastra on the Door to Understanding the Hundred Dharmas. A text fundamental to Consciousness Only doctrine, by Vasubandhu Bodhisattva, with commentary by the Venerable Master Hua. Includes lists of the Hundred Dharmas in English, Chinese, and Sanskrit for memorization. ISBN 0-88139-003-8. 130 pp. $6.50.

Song of Enlightenment. The famous lyric poem of the state of the Ch'an sage, by the Venerable Master Yung Chia of the T'ang Dynasty. ISBN 0-88139-100-X. 85 pp. $5.00.

The Ten Dharma Realms Are Not beyond a Single Thought. An eloquent poem on all the realms of being, accompanied by extensive commentarial material and drawings.
ISBN 0-917512-12-X. 72 pp. $4.00.
ISBN 0-88139-503-X. 177 pp. $8.00. Bilingual, English/Chinese

Venerable Master Hua's Talks on Dharma. Collections of talks given by the Venerable Master on various occasions. Emphasis is placed on how to apply Buddhist principles to personal cultivation. Bilingual Chinese/English.
Volume One, ISBN 0-88139-025-9. 227 pp. $7.50.
Volume Two, ISBN 0-88139-026-7. 217 pp. $7.50.
Volume Three, ISBN 0-88139-027-5. 219 pp. $7.50.
Volume Four, ISBN 0-88139-028-3. 217 pp. $7.50.

(**Khai Thị, Quyển 1.** Vietnamese translation of Volumes One & Two of *Venerable Master Hua's Talks on Dharma,* complete in one book. ISBN 0-88139-200-6. 264 pp. $10.00.)

Venerable Master Hua's Talks on Dharma during the 1993 Trip to Taiwan. Special Edition of *Talks on Dharma* series. Talks given during the Venerable Master's final visit to Taiwan. Bilingual Chinese/English. Fifteen pages of color photos.
ISBN 0-88139-023-2. 279 pp. $8.50.

Water Mirror Reflecting Heaven. An essay on the fundamental principle of cause and effect, with biographical material on contemporary Buddhist cultivation in China. Clear and to the point; very readable for young and old.
ISBN 0-88139-501-3. 82 pp. $4.00.

Biographical

In Memory of the Venerable Master Hsuan Hua. Compiled following Master. Hua's "completion of the stillness" on June 7, 1995, these books contain photos of the Master and the programs he founded as well as biographical accounts of the Master's life, essays, and poems written by the Master's disciples and others whose lives he touched. Volume Two includes photos of the cremation ceremony and other memorial ceremonies. Both volumes are bilingual Chinese/English.
Volume One, softcover, ISBN 0-88139-551-X. 249 pp. $35.00.
Volume One, hardcover, ISBN 0-88139-554-4. 249 pp. $35.00.
Volume Two, hardcover, ISBN 0-88139-553-6. 506 pp. $45.00.
Volume Three, hardcover, ISBN 0-88139-557-9. 447 pp. $40.00.

Pictorial Biography of the Venerable Master Hsü Yün. Prose and verse written by the Venerable Master Hua documenting Venerable Yün's life. Illustrated with brush drawings. Each volume contains 104 sections of prose, verse, and drawings.
Volume One, ISBN 0-88139-008-9. 120 pp.
Volume Two, ISBN 0-88139-116-6. 208 pp.
Two volume set. $16.00.

Records of High Sanghans. A living tradition is sustained to the extent that it is embodied in its heroes. The Buddhist tradition is enhanced by a large body of literature containing truly moving and inspiring life stories of Sanghans (monastics) who dedicated their bodies and lives to the preservation and propagation of the Sagely Teachings. Volume One covers the life stories of the first eminent Sanghans who brought the Buddhadharma from India to China and the adventures of those first Sanghans who withstood severe trials and hardships as they translated the first Sutras from Indian languages into Chinese.
ISBN 0-88139-012-7. 158 pp. $7.00.

Records of the Life of the Venerable Master Hsüan Hua. The life and teachings of the Venerable Master from his birth in China to the present time in America.

Volume One. Covers the Venerable Master's life in China. ISBN 0-917512-78-2. 96 pp. $5.00.

(Spanish edition—Relaciones de la Vida del Maestro Hsuan Hua, Volume 1. ISBN 0-917512-31-6. 69 pp. $8.00.)

Volume Two. Covers the events of the Master's life as he cultivated and taught in Hong Kong. Contains many photos, poems, and stories. ISBN 0-917512-10-3. 229 pp. $8.00.

Three Steps, One Bow. The daily journals of American Bhikshus Heng Ju and Heng Yo, who during 1973 and 1974 made a pilgrimage for world peace from Gold Mountain Monastery in San Francisco to Seattle, Washington, making a full prostration (kowtowing) every third step. The pilgrimage was inspired by monks in ancient China who would bow every third step for thousands of miles to a famous monastery or renowned teacher. ISBN 0-917512-18-9. 160 pp. $5.00.

World Peace Gathering. A collection of instructional talks on Buddhism commemorating the successful completion of the bowing pilgrimage of Bhikshus Heng Ju and Heng Yo. ISBN 0-917512-05-7. 128 pp. $5.00.

News from True Cultivators. The letters written by the two more recent "Three Steps, One Bow" monks, Dharma Masters Heng Sure and Heng Ch'au, during their bowing pilgrimage, addressed to the Venerable Abbot and the Assembly of the City of Ten Thousand Buddhas, are uplifting messages to those traversing the path of cultivation and inspiring exhortations to all those concerned with evolving vital and workable methods to alleviate the acute problems of our troubled times. The language is simple; the insights are profound. No one should miss reading these books!

Volume One, ISBN 0-88139-508-0. 130 pp. $6.00.

Volume Two, ISBN 0-88139-024-0. 122 pp. $6.00.

Open Your Eyes, Take a Look at the World. The journals of Bhikshus Heng Sure and Heng Ch'au and Bhikshuni Heng Tao, written during the 1978 Asia-region visit by the Venerable Master and other members of the Sino-American Buddhist Association. ISBN 0-917512-32-4. 347 pp. $9.00.

With One Heart Bowing to the City of 10,000 Buddhas. The moving journals of American Bhikshus Heng Sure and Heng Ch'au, who made a "Three Steps, One Bow" pilgrimage from Gold Wheel Temple in Los Angeles to the City of 10,000 Buddhas, located 110 miles north of San Francisco, from May 1977 to October 1979. Set $63.00.

Volume One. May 6–June 30, 1977.
ISBN 0-917512-21-9. 180 pp.
Volume Two. July 1–October 30, 1977.
ISBN 0-917512-23-5. 322 pp.
Volume Three. October 30–December 20, 1977.
ISBN 0-917512-89-8. 154 pp.
Volume Four. December 17, 1977–January 21, 1978.
ISBN 0-917512-90-1. 136 pp.
Volume Five. January 28–February 18, 1978.
ISBN 0-917512-91-X. 127 pp.
Volume Six. February 19–April 2, 1978.
ISBN 0-917512-92-8. 200 pp.
Volume Seven. April 3–May 24, 1978.
ISBN 0-917512-99-5. 160 pp.
Volume Eight. May 24-September, 1978
ISBN 0-917512-53-7. 232 pp.
Volume Nine. September–October, 1978.
ISBN 0-88139-509-9. 232 pp.

Children's Books

Cherishing Life. Contains verses and brush drawings about not taking life, and public records about cause and effect, drawn from events recorded by Dharma Masters, giving people's awareness of the reasons for their retributions in the animal realm. For elementary age children as well as adults.
Volume One, ISBN 0-88139-004-6. 150 pp. $7.00.
Volume Two, ISBN 0-88139-015-1. 150 pp. $7.00.

Human Roots: Buddhist Stories for Young Readers. Volume One has a total of fourteen stories from the Buddhist canon and historical records. ISBN 0-88139-500-5. 95 pp. $5.00.
Volume Two, ISBN 0-88139-017-8. 138 pp. $5.00.

Music, Novels, & Brochures

Songs for Awakening. Lyrics and guitar music for over forty modern American Buddhist songs. Indexed according to title and first line. With drawings, woodcuts, and photographs. The 9″ by 12″ songbook makes a fine gift to introduce your friends to Buddhism. ISBN 0-917512-63-4. 112 pp. $8.00.

Awakening. A 12″ stereo record album of ten Buddhist songs in Western style (all in English) ranging from pop and rock, to folk and country. Subjects covered include: Bodhisattva vows, the *I Ching*, Ch'an meditation, Lao-Tzu, the *Lotus Sutra,* Abhidharma meditation, and Amitabha Buddha and his Pure Land. $7.00 plus $1.00 shipping in the U.S.A. and $2.00 for international orders.

The Three Cart Patriarch. A 12″ stereo lp recorded by and for children, based on the *Monkey Tales* of China. Featuring stories, six musical productions, and many special effects. $7.00 plus $1.00 shipping in the U.S.A. and $2.00 for international orders.

City of 10,000 Buddhas Color Brochure. Over thirty color photos of the scenic center for World Buddhism, along with many poems and a description of the City's activities. 24 pp. $2.00.

Celebrisi's Journey. A novel by David Rounds describing the events in a modern American's quest for enlightenment.
(First edition) ISBN 0-917512-14-6. 178 pp. $4.00.

Heng Ch'au's Journal. An account of the remarkable experiences and changes undergone by Bhikshu Heng Ch'au when he first came in contact with Gold Mountain Monastery.
ISBN 0-88139-052-6. 20 pp. $1.95.

Ordering Information

Postage & Handling:

The following rates for postage and handling apply to orders of six or fewer books. Up to six audio tapes count as one book. On orders of more than six books, we suggest that purchasers submit their orders for a precise quote on postage and handling costs.

United States: $2.00 for the first book and $0.75 for each additional book. All publications are sent via special fourth class. Allow from two weeks to one month for delivery.

International: $2.50 for the first book and $1.50 for each additional book. All publications are sent via "book rate" or direct mail sack (surface). For countries in which parcels may be lost, we suggest orders be sent via registered mail for an additional $3.25 per parcel of ten books each. We are not responsible for parcels lost in the mail. Allow two to three months for delivery.

- California residents add 8.25% tax.
- Make checks payable to: D.R.B.A.

All orders require prepayment, including postage and handling fees, before they will be shipped to the buyer. Submit order to:

Buddhist Text Translation Society
Sagely City of Ten Thousand Buddhas
P.O. Box 217, Talmage, CA 95481-0217 USA
Phone: (707) 462-0939; Fax: (707) 462-0949

or to:

Buddhist Text Translation Society
International Translation Institute
1777 Murchison Drive, Burlingame, CA 94010-4504 USA
Phone: (650) 692-5912; Fax: (650) 692-5056

Most branches of the Dharma Realm Buddhist Association, as well as some retail booksellers, also offer Buddhist Text Translation Society publications for sale.

The Buddhist Monthly—Vajra Bodhi Sea

The Buddhist Monthly—Vajra Bodhi Sea is a monthly journal of orthodox Buddhism which has been published by the Dharma Realm Buddhist Association, formerly known as the Sino-American Buddhist Association, since 1970. Each issue contains the most recent translations of the Buddhist canon by the Buddhist Text Translation Society. Also included in each issue are a biography of a great Patriarch of Buddhism from the ancient past, sketches of the lives of contemporary monastics and lay-followers around the world, articles on practice, and other material. The journal is bilingual, Chinese and English, 48 pages in an 8½" by 11" format.

Single issue $4.00
One year subscription $40.00
Three years $100.00

ISSN 0507-6986 (Postage is included in the subscription fee.)

Send orders to:

Vajra Bodhi Sea subscriptions
800 Sacramento Street
San Francisco, CA 94108
(415) 421-6117 Fax: (415) 788-6001

Dharma Realm Buddhist Association Branches

Home Page: **http:\\www.drba.org**

Main Branch:

The City of Ten Thousand Buddhas

P.O. Box 217, Talmage, CA 95481-0217 USA
Tel: (707) 462-0939 Fax: (707) 462-0949

The City of the Dharma Realm
1029 West Capitol Avenue, West Sacramento, CA 95691 USA
Tel: (916) 374-8268

The International Translation Institute
1777 Murchison Drive, Burlingame, CA 94010-4504 USA
Tel: (650) 692-5912 Fax: (650) 692-5056

Institute for World Religions (Berkeley Buddhist Monastery)
2304 McKinley Avenue, Berkeley, CA 94703 USA
Tel: (510) 848-3440 Fax: (510) 548-4551

Gold Mountain Monastery
800 Sacramento Street, San Francisco, CA 94108 USA
Tel: (415) 421-6117 Fax: (415) 788-6001

Gold Sage Monastery
11455 Clayton Road, San Jose, CA 95127 USA
Tel: (408) 923-7243 Fax: (408) 923-1064

Gold Summit Monastery
233-1st Avenue, West Seattle, WA 98119 USA
Tel: (206) 217-9320

Gold Wheel Monastery
235 North Avenue 58, Los Angeles, CA 90042 USA
Tel: (213) 258-6668

Blessings, Prosperity, & Longevity Monastery
4140 Long Beach Boulevard, Long Beach, CA 90807 USA
Tel: (562) 595-4966

Long Beach Monastery
3361 East Ocean Boulevard, Long Beach, CA 90803 USA
Tel: (562) 438-8902

Avatamsaka Hermitage
11721 Beall Mountain Road, Potomac, MD 20854-1128 USA
Tel: (301) 299-3693

Avatamsaka Monastery
1009-4th Avenue, S.W. Calgary, AB T2P 0K8 Canada
Tel: (403) 269-2960

Gold Buddha Monastery
301 East Hastings Street, Vancouver, BC V6A 1P3 Canada
Tel: (604) 684-3754

Dharma Realm Buddhist Books Distribution Society
11th Floor, 85 Chung-hsiao E. Road, Sec. 6, Taipei, R.O.C.
Tel: (02) 786-3022

Tze Yun Tung Temple
Batu 5½, Jalan Sungai Besi, Salak Selatan
57100 Kuala Lumpur, Malaysia
Tel: (03) 782-6560 Fax: (03) 780-1272

Buddhist Lecture Hall
31 Wong Nei Chong Road, Top Floor
Happy Valley, Hong Kong
Tel: 2572-7644